FARM JOURNAL'S

FRIENDLY FOOD GIFTS
FROM YOUR KITCHEN

Other cookbooks by FARM JOURNAL

FARM JOURNAL'S

FRIENDLY FOOD GIFTS
FROM YOUR KITCHEN

By ELISE W. MANNING
FARM JOURNAL Food Editor

Recipes selected and edited by
PATRICIA A. WARD
Assistant Food Editor

Food gift containers designed by
MAUREEN SWEENEY
Farm Journal Art Staff

Photography supervised by
ALFRED CASCIATO
Farm Journal Associate Art Director

Doubleday & Company, Inc.
Garden City, New York

Library of Congress Cataloging in Publication Data

Main entry under title:

Farm journal's friendly food gifts from your kitchen.

Includes index.
1. Cookery.   2. Gifts.   I. Manning, Elise W.
II. Farm journal (Philadelphia, 1956–   )
III. Title: Friendly food gifts from your kitchen.
TX715.F2244   641.5
ISBN: 0-385-13520-3
Library of Congress Catalog Card Number 77–94865

CONTENTS

COLOR ILLUSTRATIONS

Color photographs by: William Hazzard/Hazzard Studios, Meillier/McCune and Charles P. Mills.

Introduction

THE NICEST GIFT OF ALL . . . A HOMEMADE SPECIALTY FROM YOUR KITCHEN

Gifts of homemade food are part of the American heritage. And they play a big role in farm communities. We decided to ask farm women just when they gave foods as a gift, what kind of food they gave and how the food was packaged.

Letters and recipes poured into *Farm Journal*'s food department. We discovered that the range of food gift situations covered a great many more occasions than the familiar Christmas and hostess gifts.

We took all of the farm women's ideas and divided them into eight chapters and added a ninth on creative ways to package the gifts.

The first chapter contains some of the best casseroles from farm kitchens as well as homemade rolls and mixes. These are popular choices to give to a new neighbor who is too busy settling in and hasn't finished unpacking all the pots and pans.

In the second chapter you will find some great dishes to take to a friend who has just arrived home from the hospital—casseroles that are sturdy family fare as well as little surprises to brighten a dreary afternoon.

If you are looking for birthday present ideas, turn to Chapter

3 and try a luscious birthday cake, complete birthday meals or a main dish especially suited to the man in the family.

When there is a death in the community, farm women know that good comforting food is appreciated by the bereaved family. Chapter 4 is filled with down-to-earth casseroles and salads as well as cakes that can be baked and served in the same pan.

In Chapter 5 there are some unique gifts to give a hostess or to thank a friend that has lent a helping hand when you have needed it. Many of these gifts can be made ahead to have on hand when you are invited out to dinner or want to give a spur-of-the-moment gift.

Elderly people who live alone or who can't get around too easily really appreciate a visit and a thoughtful homemade food gift. In Chapter 6 we share farm women's favorite recipes that they give to shut-ins or to friends in nursing homes.

For all those special holidays throughout the year, we have some delicious recipes to make and give—treats for Halloween, splendid foods for Easter giving, Valentine remembrances for friends and relatives both near and far away. Mother's Day and Father's Day can be extra special if you make and give one of the recipes in Chapter 7.

All the people on your Christmas list will be delighted to receive any one of the gifts in Chapter 8. There are spectacular homemade breads, mouth-watering candies and tangy relishes.

The very last chapter tells you how to make creative containers for your food gifts. There are containers for every occasion and for every age. And many of them use everyday boxes that are found around the home. All are inexpensive to make and fun to give.

We have enjoyed testing, tasting and perfecting all the recipes in this book and we hope you will find a treasure trove of gift foods to share with your friends and neighbors.

Chapter 1

WELCOME TO OUR NEIGHBORHOOD

"I'll never forget the day we moved into our new house," a farm wife from Kansas told us. "It was a cold winter day and the snow was coming down in a thick blanket. We were tired, hungry and homesick. The doorbell rang and there in the doorway stood our next-door neighbor with a big pot of soup and homemade sandwiches. She had even brought plastic mugs and paper plates and napkins—just in case we hadn't finished unpacking our china. Suddenly the world seemed brighter. Ever since, I have always welcomed a new neighbor with a homemade meal or snack."

We have compiled recipes from farm women all over the country along with their ideas for saying "Welcome to our community."

The ideas range from full-course meals to give a weary woman a lift to a much appreciated afternoon break complete with homemade coffee and a snack.

HEARTY LUNCH FOR HUNGRY NEWCOMERS

An Iowa farm woman always bakes her Whole Wheat Sandwich Buns when she knows there is a new family in the neighborhood. In addition she makes up her children's favorite bologna spread and a quick and easy dessert, Fresh Fruit Slush. Just before noon, she piles everything into a big wicker basket, writes a welcoming note and leaves it at the door of the new neighbor, along with a bouquet of flowers from her garden.

"We raise our own lambs, so I always have plenty of frozen meat in the freezer to make this hearty Lamb Noodle Soup to surprise a new neighbor," says a Colorado ranch woman. She usually makes a double batch and puts half of it in freezer containers so that the new family can have another meal without work. Along with the soup, she takes garlic bread hot and crusty from the oven. "And a quart of my homemade applesauce for dessert," she says. "My soup always makes a big hit and everyone wants my recipe so that they, too, can greet a new neighbor."

WHOLE WHEAT SANDWICH BUNS

These buns are perfect for hamburgers or sloppy joes, too

2 c. water	2 pkgs. active dry yeast
½ c. sugar	3 eggs
½ c. nonfat dry milk	3½ c. stirred whole wheat
1 tblsp. salt	flour
¾ c. cooking oil	Milk
4½ to 5 c. sifted all-purpose	
flour	

Combine water, sugar, dry milk, salt and oil in saucepan. Heat to warm (120–130°). Stir together 4 c. all-purpose flour and yeast in bowl. Add warm liquid and eggs. Beat with electric mixer at low speed ½ minute, scraping bowl constantly. Beat at high speed 3 minutes, scraping bowl occasionally. Stir in whole wheat flour by hand. Add enough remaining all-purpose flour to make a moderately soft dough.

Knead on floured surface until smooth and elastic, about 5 minutes.

Place in greased bowl, turning to grease top. Cover and let rise in a warm place until doubled, about 1½ hours.

Punch down dough. Divide in thirds. Cover and let rest 5 minutes. Divide each third into 8 portions. Shape into balls. Place on greased baking sheets; press down with palm of hand to make 3½" rounds. Cover and let rise until doubled, 30 to 45 minutes. Brush with milk.

Bake in 375° oven 12 minutes or until golden brown. Remove from baking sheets; cool on racks. Makes 24.

HEARTY BOLOGNA SPREAD

A great budget stretcher that can be made in just minutes

1½ lbs. regular bologna, ground (about 4½ c.)
¾ c. pickle relish
3 tblsp. minced onion
1 tblsp. Worcestershire sauce
1½ c. salad dressing
12 slices process American cheese
Lettuce leaves

Combine bologna, pickle relish, onion, Worcestershire sauce and salad dressing in bowl; mix well. Spread mixture on bun or on slice of bread. Top with cheese slice and then lettuce leaf. Makes 4½ c. sandwich spread or fills 12 buns.

FRESH FRUIT SLUSH

A colorful fruit combo that is also refreshing served without freezing. Just chill and serve on lettuce leaves

4 large navel oranges
2 c. sliced fresh strawberries
1 c. seedless green grapes
3 medium bananas, sliced
1 (6 oz.) can frozen lemonade, slightly thawed

Peel oranges with sharp knife removing the white part of peel. Using a knife, cut orange segments from membranes into bowl. After removing all the segments, squeeze membranes releasing juice into bowl.

Add strawberries, grapes, bananas and lemonade; toss lightly to mix. Spoon into serving dishes or plastic cups. Cover with aluminum foil. Freeze until slightly icy, about 1¼ hours. Makes about 8 cups.

Note: Fruit salad can be made the day before and refrigerated. Freeze 1¼ hours before serving.

LAMB NOODLE SOUP

Well-flavored soup that is also good made with beef chuck

2½ lbs. lamb shoulder, cut in 1½" thick slices	½ tsp. thyme leaves
2 tblsp. cooking oil	¼ tsp. rosemary leaves
2 c. chopped celery	¼ tsp. pepper
1 c. chopped onion	1 bay leaf
1 clove garlic, minced	6 oz. wide noodles (4c.)
7 c. water	⅓ c. chopped fresh parsley
1 tblsp. salt	Sliced green onions and tops

Remove most of the fat from lamb. Brown lamb in hot oil in 4-qt. Dutch oven. Remove lamb as it browns. Add celery, onion and garlic; sauté until lightly browned. Add lamb, water, salt, thyme, rosemary, pepper and bay leaf. Bring to a boil; reduce heat. Skim off foam. Cover and simmer 2 hours.

Remove lamb from broth. Bring broth to a boil. Add noodles. Cover and cook 15 minutes or until tender.

Meanwhile, remove meat from bones. Add meat and parsley to broth. Serve in bowls topped with green onions. Makes 2 quarts.

JUST THOUGHT YOU'D LIKE A HOT SUPPER

A big pot of chili seems to be a popular dish for farm women to make and give to neighbors who are busy settling in to new surroundings. It's hearty and just about everyone likes chili—especially teen-agers.

A Nebraska farm woman likes to give a new neighbor "something a little special," so she bakes her Cheese and Bacon Pie and always includes a big tossed salad, made with vegetables from her garden.

"I found from experience that Franks in Corn Blankets are most welcome as a meal to take to a new neighbor," a South Dakota farm woman told us. "Members of my family are always delighted when a new neighbor moves into town, because they know they will have Franks in Corn Blankets for supper, too!"

GROUND BEEF CHILI

Serve this mildly seasoned chili topped with shredded cheese

2 lbs. ground beef	⅛ tsp. pepper
1 c. chopped onion	1½ tblsp. chili powder
1 c. chopped celery	4 c. tomato juice
1 c. chopped green pepper	2 (1 lb.) cans kidney beans
1 clove garlic, minced	2 (1 lb.) cans tomatoes, cut
1 tsp. salt	up

Cook ground beef in 6-qt. Dutch oven. When meat begins to turn color, add onion, celery, green pepper, garlic, salt, pepper and chili powder. Cook until mixture is well browned.

Add tomato juice, undrained kidney beans and tomatoes. Bring to a boil; reduce heat. Simmer, uncovered, 45 minutes. Makes about 3 quarts.

QUICK CHILI BEANS

"I made up this recipe one night when I needed a covered dish for a meeting. It made a big hit," a Texas woman wrote us

1 (15 oz.) can chili without beans	1 (5½ oz.) bag tortilla chips
1 (1 lb.) can barbecue-style beans	¾ c. chopped onion
	2 c. shredded Longhorn cheese

Combine chili without beans and barbecue beans in bowl. Set aside.

Crumble ⅓ of tortilla chips in bottom of greased 1½-qt. glass loaf dish. Spoon ½ of chili bean mixture over chips. Sprinkle with ½ of onion and ½ of cheese. Top with ⅓ of crumbled tortilla chips. Repeat layers, ending with tortilla chips.

Bake in 350° oven 30 minutes or until hot. Makes 4 servings.

CHEESE AND BACON PIE

This cheese pie makes a great snack served warm or cold

4 large shredded wheat biscuits, crushed (1½ c.)	½ tsp. salt
3 tblsp. melted butter or regular margarine	1/16 tsp. pepper
6 strips bacon	1½ c. milk
3 eggs	2 c. shredded Cheddar cheese
	Paprika

Combine crushed wheat biscuits and butter in bowl; mix well. Press wheat biscuit mixture into greased 9" pie plate.

Fry bacon in skillet until crisp. Remove and drain on paper towels. Crumble bacon; set aside.

Beat together eggs, salt, pepper and milk in bowl with rotary beater until well blended. Place ½ of bacon in wheat biscuit shell. Top with 1 c. of the cheese. Arrange remaining bacon on top. Pour egg mixture evenly over all. Top with remaining 1 c. cheese. Sprinkle with paprika.

Bake in 350° oven 40 minutes or until golden brown. Makes 6 servings.

FRANKS IN CORN BLANKETS

Special way to serve franks . . . so much better than buns

1 c. unsifted flour	½ c. milk
½ c. cornmeal	½ c. ketchup
2 tsp. baking powder	2 tblsp. prepared mustard
1 tsp. salt	2 tblsp. pickle relish
⅓ c. shortening	8 frankfurters
1 c. shredded Cheddar cheese	

Sift together flour, cornmeal, baking powder and salt into mixing bowl. Cut in shortening with pastry blender or two knives until mixture resembles coarse crumbs. Stir in cheese.

Add milk, stirring just until ingredients are moistened. Roll out dough on floured surface to 16×7″ rectangle. Cut into 8 (4×3½″) rectangles.

Combine ketchup, mustard and pickle relish in small bowl. Spread over rectangles. (Serve any remaining sauce with franks.) Place a frankfurter on dough rectangle. Wrap dough around it; press to seal edge. Place seam side down on ungreased baking sheets.

Bake in 425° oven 15 minutes or until golden brown. Makes 8 servings.

SAY WELCOME WITH A MAIN DISH DINNER

Main dishes for dinner are a big favorite for giving to a new neighbor. Farm homemakers often make and freeze several casseroles ahead. "Even if we're in the midst of harvesting our corn, I have a casserole handy to pull from the freezer when a new neighbor arrives," a Nebraska woman told us. A popular addition is a big basket of home-grown vegetables to go along with the main dish. One farm wife gives a big head of cabbage from her garden—with a jar of homemade coleslaw dressing.

MEATBALL AND BEAN STEW

Meatball and kidney bean combination enhanced with Italian seasoning . . . certain to please the heartiest appetite

1 lb. ground beef	1 c. green pepper strips
½ c. soft bread crumbs	2 (1 lb. 1 oz.) cans kidney
¼ c. minced onion	beans
3 tblsp. minced fresh parsley	1 (1 lb. 12 oz.) can Italian
1 tsp. salt	tomatoes, cut up
½ tsp. oregano leaves	1 (15 oz.) can tomato sauce
¼ tsp. basil leaves	1 bay leaf
1 egg	½ tsp. oregano leaves
¼ c. milk	¼ tsp. basil leaves
2 tblsp. cooking oil	Shredded Cheddar cheese

Combine ground beef, bread crumbs, onion, parsley, salt, ½ tsp. oregano, ¼ tsp. basil, egg and milk in bowl. Mix lightly, but well. Shape into 32 meatballs. Brown in hot oil in Dutch oven; remove meatballs as they brown. Pour off all but 2 tblsp. fat.

Sauté green pepper in 2 tblsp. fat until tender (do not

brown). Add kidney beans, tomatoes, tomato sauce, bay leaf, ½ tsp. oregano and ¼ tsp. basil; mix well. Add meatballs. Bring mixture to a boil; reduce heat. Simmer, uncovered, 30 minutes. Serve in bowls topped with Cheddar cheese. Makes 10 servings.

PIZZA MEAT LOAF

Children will love this moist loaf that tastes like pizza

2 lbs. ground lean beef	1 small clove garlic, minced
1 c. soft bread crumbs	1½ tsp. oregano leaves
1 c. shredded mozzarella cheese	1 tsp. salt
½ c. finely diced cooked ham	¼ tsp. pepper
	2 eggs, slightly beaten
2 tblsp. minced fresh parsley	½ c. tomato juice

Combine all ingredients in large bowl. Mix lightly, but well. Shape mixture into 12″ loaf on greased 15½ × 10½ × 1″ jelly roll pan.

Bake in 350° oven 50 minutes or until done. Let stand 5 minutes before slicing. Makes 6 to 8 servings.

WELCOME NEIGHBOR CASSEROLE

Attractive hot dish made from basic kitchen ingredients

1½ lbs. ground beef	⅓ c. uncooked regular rice
1½ c. chopped onion	1 (1 lb.) can red kidney beans
2 c. chopped celery	
2 tsp. chili powder	1 (10¾ oz.) can condensed tomato soup
¼ tsp. pepper	1¼ c. water
2 c. thinly sliced pared potatoes	2 beef bouillon cubes

Cook ground beef in 12″ skillet until it begins to change color. Add onion, celery, chili powder and pepper. Cook until mixture is well browned. Remove excess fat.

Add potatoes, rice, undrained kidney beans, tomato soup, water and beef bouillon cubes. Bring mixture to a boil. Pour into 3-qt. casserole. Cover.

Bake in 350° oven 40 minutes or until potatoes are tender. Makes 10 servings.

BEAN AND BEEF LASAGNA

An outstanding casserole with a creamy rich sauce made with cream cheese and sour cream sparked with green onions

8 oz. medium noodles
1 lb. ground beef
1 c. sliced green onions and
   tops
1 clove garlic, minced
1 (1 lb.) can red kidney
   beans, drained and
   mashed
2 (8 oz.) cans tomato sauce
2 tblsp. chopped fresh
   parsley

1 tsp. sugar
½ tsp. salt
¼ tsp. pepper
1 (8 oz.) pkg. cream cheese,
   softened
2 c. dairy sour cream
1 c. shredded Cheddar
   cheese

Cook noodles in boiling salted water in Dutch oven until almost tender. Drain. Rinse with cold water. Drain well.

Cook ground beef in 10″ skillet until meat begins to turn color. Add green onions and garlic; cook until mixture is well browned. Pour off excess fat. Add mashed beans, tomato sauce, parsley, sugar, salt and pepper; mix well. Bring mixture to a boil. Reduce heat and simmer 10 minutes. Remove from heat.

Arrange noodles in greased 13×9×2″ baking dish. Combine cream cheese and sour cream in bowl. Beat with electric mixer at medium speed until smooth and creamy. Spread over noodles. Top with meat mixture. Cover dish with aluminum foil.

Bake in 350° oven 30 minutes or until bubbling around edges. Remove aluminum foil. Sprinkle with cheese. Return to oven; bake long enough to melt cheese. Makes 8 servings.

TEXAS MEAL-IN-ONE

A perfect budget meal for eight . . . serve with tossed salad

2 medium carrots, pared and shredded	2 beef bouillon cubes
1 medium onion, chopped (½ c.)	2 c. boiling water
½ c. chopped celery	1 c. uncooked regular rice
3 tblsp. cooking oil	2 c. tomato juice
1½ lbs. ground beef	2 tblsp. tomato paste
1 tsp. salt	1 (1 lb.) can whole kernel corn
¼ tsp. pepper	2 tblsp. chopped fresh parsley
¼ tsp. cayenne pepper	

Sauté carrots, onion and celery in hot oil in 12″ skillet until tender (do not brown). Add ground beef, salt, pepper and cayenne pepper. Cook until meat is well browned.

Dissolve bouillon cubes in boiling water. Add bouillon, rice, tomato juice, tomato paste and undrained corn to skillet. Stir well; bring mixture to a boil. Reduce heat and cover. Simmer 30 minutes or until rice is tender. Top with parsley before serving. Makes 8 servings.

HERBED COLESLAW DRESSING

An unusual herbed cabbage dressing . . . keeps for two months

1 c. minced onion	½ tsp. thyme leaves
2 c. sugar	½ tsp. basil leaves
1 c. vinegar	½ tsp. rosemary leaves
4 tsp. salt	½ tsp. marjoram leaves
2 tsp. dry mustard	½ tsp. oregano leaves
2 tsp. celery seeds	1 qt. salad oil
½ tsp. pepper	

Combine onion, sugar and vinegar in mixing bowl. Add salt, dry mustard, celery seeds, pepper, thyme, basil, rosemary, marjoram and oregano. Gradually add oil, beating with electric mixer at medium speed, until mixture is thickened and sugar is dissolved. Pour into jars. Cover tightly. Store in refrigerator. Serve over shredded cabbage. You will need approximately ½ c. dressing for 4 c. shredded cabbage. Makes 2 quarts.

THE COFFEE BREAK

"When we moved into a new town," a Minnesota farm woman said, "we were so pleased when our neighbors dropped in with coffee and coffee cake in the middle of the afternoon. So now, I always do this for our newcomers."

We have included coffee-break favorites from farm women from light-as-air doughnuts to an heirloom chewy cookie. One farm wife suggested that it's a welcome touch if you bring a big thermos of hot cocoa for the youngsters as well as coffee for adults.

CRUSTY BROWN SUGAR COFFEE CAKE

Better make two . . . your family is sure to like it, too

2 c. sifted flour	2 eggs
1 tsp. baking powder	1 tsp. vanilla
1 tsp. baking soda	1 c. buttermilk
½ tsp. salt	⅓ c. brown sugar, firmly
½ c. butter or regular	packed
margarine	¼ c. sugar
1 c. sugar	1 tsp. ground cinnamon

Sift together flour, baking powder, baking soda and salt.

Cream together butter and 1 c. sugar in mixing bowl until light and fluffy, using electric mixer at medium speed. Add eggs, one at a time, beating well after each addition. Beat in vanilla.

Add dry ingredients alternately with buttermilk, beating well after each addition. Spread batter in greased 13✕9✕2″ baking pan.

Combine brown sugar, ¼ c. sugar and cinnamon in bowl; mix well. Sprinkle over batter.

Bake in 350° oven 30 minutes or until golden brown. Cut in squares and serve warm. Makes 16 servings.

SOUR CREAM WALNUT COFFEE CAKE

An excellent tender-crumbed coffee cake to serve with mugs of hot spiced apple cider on a crisp autumn day

2 c. sifted flour	1 c. dairy sour cream
1 tsp. baking powder	1 tsp. baking soda
½ tsp. salt	3 tblsp. brown sugar, firmly
½ c. butter or regular	packed
margarine	2 tblsp. sugar
1 c. sugar	½ tsp. ground cinnamon
2 eggs	½ c. chopped walnuts
1 tsp. vanilla	

Sift together flour, baking powder and salt.

Cream together butter and 1 c. sugar in mixing bowl until light and fluffy, using electric mixer at medium speed. Add eggs, one at a time, beating well after each addition. Beat in vanilla.

Combine sour cream and baking soda in small bowl. Add dry ingredients alternately with sour cream mixture, beating well after each addition. Spread batter in greased 13×9×2" baking pan.

Combine brown sugar, 2 tblsp. sugar, cinnamon and walnuts in small bowl; mix well. Sprinkle over batter.

Bake in 325° oven 35 minutes or until golden brown. Cut in squares and serve warm. Makes 16 servings.

SUNNY CITRUS MUFFINS

Quick-to-fix muffins that are sure to please everyone

2 c. regular or buttermilk pancake mix	2 tblsp. melted shortening
⅓ c. wheat germ	1 c. milk
¼ c. sugar	1 tsp. grated lemon rind
1 egg, beaten	1 tsp. grated orange rind

Combine pancake mix, wheat germ and sugar in mixing bowl.

Combine egg, shortening, milk, lemon rind and orange rind; blend well. Add to dry ingredients, stirring just enough to moisten. Spoon batter into 12 well-greased 3" muffin-pan cups, filling two thirds full.

Bake in 425° oven 20 minutes or until done. Serve warm. Makes 12 muffins.

SUGARED YEAST DOUGHNUTS

These doughnuts are also good frosted with confectioners sugar icing and rolled in flaked coconut or chocolate jimmies

1 c. milk, scalded
⅓ c. cooking oil
3 tblsp. sugar
1½ tsp. salt
2 pkgs. active dry yeast
¼ c. lukewarm water
  (110°)

1 egg
4 c. sifted flour
Cooking oil
½ c. sugar
½ tsp. ground cinnamon

Combine milk, ⅓ c. oil, 3 tblsp. sugar and salt in mixing bowl. Cook to lukewarm.

Sprinkle yeast on lukewarm water; stir to dissolve. Add yeast, mixture, egg and 1 c. flour to milk mixture. Beat with electric mixer at medium speed until smooth, about 2 minutes, scraping bowl occasionally. Or beat with spoon until batter is smooth.

Gradually add remaining flour, blending well. Roll out dough to ½" thickness on floured surface. Cut with floured doughnut cutter; place on floured waxed paper. Cover and let rise in a warm place until doubled, about 1 hour.

Pour oil into skillet or deep fat fryer, filling one third full. Heat oil to 350°. Slide doughnuts into hot oil using floured pancake turner. Fry until golden brown, turning once. Drain on paper towels. Roll doughnuts in combined ½ c. sugar and cinnamon. Doughnuts are good served warm. Makes 18 doughnuts.

GRANDMOTHER'S CHOCOLATE CHIPPERS

These chewy cookies are perfect with cups of hot cocoa

1 c. butter or regular margarine
1 c. brown sugar, firmly packed
½ c. sugar
1 tsp. vanilla
2 eggs
2½ c. sifted flour
1 tsp. baking soda
1 tsp. salt
1 c. semi-sweet chocolate pieces

Cream together butter, brown sugar and sugar in mixing bowl until light and fluffy, using electric mixer at medium speed. Beat in vanilla. Add eggs, one at a time, beating well after each addition.

Sift together flour, baking soda and salt. Stir into creamed mixture; blend well. Stir in chocolate pieces. Drop mixture by teaspoonfuls, about 2″ apart, on greased baking sheets.

Bake in 375° oven 8 to 10 minutes or until golden brown. Remove from baking sheets; cool on racks. Makes 4½ dozen.

TWO GIFTS IN ONE

A great many farm women prefer to make their own convenience mixes instead of buying them at the store. First of all they taste better. And in most cases they are less expensive. When a new family has moved into the neighborhood, a very popular gift is a big basket of homemade muffins, biscuits or cake made from a homemade mix. In addition to the baked goods, many farm wives take along a big apothecary jar filled with the dry mix and a little note attached that says "welcome," plus a recipe or two for using the mix.

BISCUIT MIX

An empty shortening can covered with self-adhesive plastic or wrapping paper is the perfect gift container for this mix

8 c. sifted flour	4 tsp. salt
1 c. nonfat dry milk	1⅓ c. shortening
¼ c. baking powder	

Sift together flour, dry milk, baking powder and salt 3 times. Place dry ingredients into large mixing bowl. Cut in shortening with pastry blender or two knives until mixture is crumbly. Store in tightly closed container. Makes about 12 cups.

Directions to pack with mix: Store Biscuit Mix in cool place up to 3 months. Use mix to make Hot Biscuits and Orange Pinwheels (recipes follow).

HOT BISCUITS

3 c. Biscuit Mix
⅔ to ¾ c. water

Combine Biscuit Mix with enough water in bowl to make a soft dough. Stir about 25 strokes. Turn onto lightly floured surface; knead lightly 10 times. Roll dough to ½" thickness. Cut into rounds with floured 2" cutter. Place biscuits, about 1" apart, on greased baking sheets.

Bake in 425° oven 12 to 15 minutes or until browned. Serve at once. Makes 15.

ORANGE PINWHEELS

3 c. Biscuit Mix	2 tsp. grated orange rind
⅔ to ¾ c. water	1 tblsp. melted butter or
½ c. sugar	regular margarine
⅓ c. melted butter or	
regular margarine	

Combine Biscuit Mix with enough water in bowl to make a soft dough. Stir about 25 strokes. Turn onto lightly floured surface; knead lightly 10 times. Roll dough to 18×8" rectangle.

Combine sugar, ⅓ c. melted butter and orange rind in bowl; blend well. Spread over dough. Roll up like jelly roll, starting at long side. Pinch edges to seal. Cut in 1" slices. Place in greased muffin-pan cups. Brush tops with 1 tblsp. melted butter.

Bake in 400° oven 15 to 20 minutes. Serve warm. Makes 18.

QUICK BREAD MIX

Give a pack of attractive recipe cards with this mix . . . be sure to include the following recipes for muffins and waffles

8 c. sifted flour	¼ c. baking powder
1⅓ c. nonfat dry milk	3 tsp. salt
1 c. sugar	1 c. shortening

Sift together flour, dry milk, sugar, baking powder and salt 3 times. Place in large bowl. Cut in shortening with pastry blender or two knives until well mixed. Store in tightly covered container in cool place. Can be stored up to 1 month. Makes 12 cups.

Directions to pack with mix: Store Quick Bread Mix in a cool place. It keeps up to 1 month. Use mix to make Speedy Muffins and Speedy Waffles (recipes follow).

SPEEDY MUFFINS

3 c. Quick Bread Mix
1 c. water
1 egg, beaten

Combine Quick Bread Mix, water and egg in bowl. Stir about 15 strokes. Batter will be lumpy. Spoon batter into greased 2½" muffin-pan cups, filling two thirds full.

Bake in 425° oven 18 to 20 minutes or until golden brown. Serve warm. Makes 12.

SPEEDY WAFFLES

3 c. Quick Bread Mix
1½ c. water
1 egg, separated

Combine Quick Bread Mix, water and egg yolk in bowl. Stir just enough to mix.

Beat egg white in small bowl until stiff peaks form. Fold into waffle batter. Bake on heated greased waffle iron. Makes 12 (4") waffles.

BROWNIE MIX

Why not bake a batch of Short-cut Brownies to include with the Brownie Mix . . . sure to please a new neighbor

4 c. sifted flour	**4 tsp. baking powder**
8 c. sugar	**4 tsp. salt**
2½ c. baking cocoa	**2 c. shortening**

Sift together flour, sugar, cocoa, baking powder and salt into large bowl. Cut in shortening with pastry blender or two knives until well blended. Store in covered container in cool place or in refrigerator. Makes 16 cups.

Directions to pack with mix: Store Brownie Mix in cool place or in refrigerator up to 3 months. Use mix to make Fudge Sauce, Short-cut Brownies and Quick Brownie Cake (recipes follow).

FUDGE SAUCE

1 c. Brownie Mix
½ c. water

Combine Brownie Mix and water in saucepan. Cook over medium heat, stirring constantly, until mixture boils. Reduce heat and cover. Simmer until sauce is thick and smooth. Cool slightly. Serve over ice cream.

SHORT-CUT BROWNIES

2 c. Brownie Mix   1 tsp. vanilla
2 eggs, beaten   ½ c. chopped walnuts

Combine Brownie Mix, eggs and vanilla in bowl; blend well. Mixture will not be smooth. Stir in walnuts. Spread mixture in greased 8″ square baking pan.

Bake in 350° oven 20 to 25 minutes or until a slight imprint remains when lightly touched with finger. Cool in pan on rack. Cut in 2″ squares. Makes 16.

QUICK BROWNIE CAKE

2 c. Brownie Mix   1 tsp. vanilla
3 tblsp. milk   Ice cream
3 eggs, separated

Combine Brownie Mix, milk, egg yolks and vanilla in bowl. Stir until blended. Beat egg whites in bowl until stiff peaks form, using electric mixer at high speed. Fold into batter. Spread batter in greased and waxed paper-lined 8″ square baking pan.

Bake in 350° oven 35 minutes or until done. Cool in pan on rack 10 minutes. Remove from pan; cool on rack. Cut in squares and top with ice cream. Makes 9 servings.

INSTANT COCOA MIX

For a complete gift, include a bag of miniature marshmallows and some handsome cocoa mugs with the instant cocoa mix

6⅔ c. nonfat dry milk or	1 c. baking cocoa
5 (1 qt.) envs.	¼ tsp. salt
1¼ c. sugar	

Sift together dry milk, sugar, baking cocoa and salt twice. Store in tightly covered container in cool dry place. Can be stored up to 3 months. Stir before using. Makes about 8 cups.

Directions to pack with mix: Store Instant Cocoa Mix in a cool dry place up to 3 months. Stir mix before using. Measure ⅓ c. Instant Cocoa Mix into 6-oz. cup. Fill with hot water; stir to blend thoroughly. For extra nutrition, substitute milk for water.

Chapter 2

TO CHEER A SICK FRIEND

"I was flat on my back for several months after a long hospital siege. I never had to worry about meals for my family. Friends and neighbors were wonderful to us. Hot casseroles, skillet suppers and homemade soup appeared every day along with a cheery message." The grateful Minnesota farm woman who wrote these words has never forgotten how much it meant to her to have neighbors bring gifts of food when she was ill, and she keeps a file of recipes to make and give to families who need a helping hand.

When a friend is feeling better but still confined to bed and a neighbor arrives with a plate of homemade rolls warm from the oven along with a jar of homemade jam or jelly, it helps to brighten a tedious day.

Youngsters especially find convalescence tiresome, and are thrilled when a neighbor brings a meal or a snack just for them. And they like it even better if there is a little present to go along with it!

We have some lovely foods to cheer up a sick person. Some are delicious, hearty casseroles and soups while others are little thoughts to show you care.

BUBBLING HOT MEALS WHEN MOTHER CAN'T COOK

Rib-sticking casseroles, a big pot of homemade soup or a skillet supper are some of the most thoughtful food gifts to give when you know the woman of the house is ill. A good home-cooked meal is also much appreciated by a young mother who has just arrived home from the hospital with a new baby.

Farm cooks have some of the best recipes in the country for one-dish meals. We share some of them with you in this section, as well as salad dressing recipes in case you want to send along some greens.

"Whenever I hear a neighbor is sick, I double my casserole recipe, serve one for supper and take the other to the needy household," wrote a South Dakota woman. "Sometimes I spend a morning making four or five casseroles to freeze and have on hand for emergencies."

We received the following note from a grateful dairy farmer's wife from Wisconsin: "The day I arrived home from the hospital, a neighbor called to tell me she was bringing a surprise meal for the family at five o'clock. That was the nicest gift anyone could have given me. The casserole arrived wrapped in aluminum foil and several thicknesses of newspaper to keep it piping hot. And she included a big bowl of freshly washed salad greens from her garden and a jar of homemade salad dressing."

EASY BEEF/VEGETABLE SOUP

Homemade soup in less than an hour. This hearty vegetable soup is so simple to prepare and so delicious

2 lbs. ground beef	4 beef bouillon cubes
2 c. chopped celery	1 (1 lb. 1 oz.) can whole
1 c. chopped onion	kernel corn
½ c. chopped green pepper	2 (10¾ oz.) cans condensed
1 clove garlic, minced	tomato soup
½ tsp. paprika	4 c. water
¼ tsp. pepper	

Cook ground beef in 6-qt. Dutch oven. When meat begins to turn color, add celery, onion, green pepper and garlic. Cook until mixture is well browned. Drain off excess fat. Add paprika, pepper, beef bouillon cubes, undrained corn, tomato soup and water. Bring to a boil; reduce heat. Cover and simmer 45 minutes. Makes 3 quarts.

MEATBALL/BEAN SKILLET

Great flavor combination . . . meatballs and baked beans in a sauce spiked with mustard and ketchup

1 lb. ground beef	1 tblsp. cooking oil
⅔ c. soft bread crumbs	1 c. chopped onion
2 tblsp. chopped fresh	2 (1 lb.) cans pork and
parsley	beans in tomato sauce
1 tsp. salt	¼ c. ketchup
⅛ tsp. pepper	2 tsp. dry mustard
¼ c. evaporated milk	

Combine ground beef, bread crumbs, parsley, salt, pepper and evaporated milk in bowl. Mix lightly, but well. Shape mixture into 18 meatballs.

Brown meatballs on all sides in hot oil in 10″ skillet. Remove meatballs as they brown. Pour off excess fat, reserving 1 tblsp. Add onion to 1 tblsp. fat in skillet. Sauté onion until tender (do not brown). Add beans, ketchup, mustard and meatballs. Heat thoroughly. Makes 6 servings.

EASY MACARONI SKILLET

"Tastes even better when reheated," says an Iowa farm woman

1 lb. ground beef
¾ c. chopped onion
½ tsp. salt
⅛ tsp. pepper
1 (1 lb.) can red kidney
   beans
1 (10¾ oz.) can condensed
   tomato soup
½ c. ketchup

¾ c. elbow macaroni
3 strips bacon, cooked,
   drained and crumbled
2 tsp. chili powder
1⅓ c. water
4 oz. process cheese spread,
   cut in ½″ cubes

Cook ground beef in 12″ skillet until meat begins to turn color. Add onion, salt and pepper. Cook until meat is well browned. Pour off excess fat.

Add undrained kidney beans, tomato soup, ketchup, uncooked macaroni, bacon, chili powder and water; mix well. Bring mixture to a boil; reduce heat. Cover and simmer 25 minutes or until macaroni is tender, stirring occasionally. Stir in cheese and serve. Makes 6 servings.

HAM AND PORK LOAF

Great way to use leftover ham . . . a delightful flavor combo

1 lb. ground cooked ham
1 lb. ground pork
2 c. cooked regular rice
½ c. finely chopped onion
1 tblsp. minced fresh parsley
1 tsp. salt

¼ tsp. pepper
¼ tsp. ground cloves
2 eggs, slightly beaten
½ c. milk
Mustard/Egg Sauce (recipe
   follows)

Combine ham, pork, rice, onion, parsley, salt, pepper, cloves, eggs and milk in large bowl. Mix lightly, but well. Shape into a 10″ loaf on a greased 15½×10½×1″ jelly roll pan.

Bake in 350° oven 1 hour 15 minutes or until done. Let stand 5 minutes before serving. Serve meat loaf with Mustard/Egg Sauce. Makes 6 to 8 servings.

Mustard/Egg Sauce: Prepare 2 c. of your favorite medium white sauce. Add 2 chopped hard-cooked eggs and 1 tsp. dry mustard. Heat well.

DINNER IN A DISH

A lightly seasoned hot dish that will tempt the palate of a convalescing person . . . so easy to digest, too

3 c. stiff, hot mashed
   potatoes*
1 egg, beaten
1 lb. ground beef
½ c. chopped onion
2 tblsp. chopped fresh
   parsley
1 tsp. marjoram leaves

½ tsp. salt
¼ tsp. pepper
2 tblsp. flour
1 (1 lb.) can tomatoes, cut
   up
½ c. ketchup
2 beef bouillon cubes
1½ c. frozen peas, thawed

Combine mashed potatoes with egg; set aside.

Cook ground beef, onion, parsley, marjoram, salt and pepper in 10″ skillet until well browned. Remove excess fat. Stir in flour. Add tomatoes, ketchup, crumbled beef bouillon cubes and peas. Bring to a boil. Pour into 2-qt. casserole. Top with potato mixture.

Bake in 350° oven 35 minutes or until potatoes are golden brown. Makes 8 servings.

*Note: Fresh or instant mashed potatoes can be used. If instant potatoes are used, prepare according to package directions for 6 servings, adding additional dry flakes to make stiff potatoes.

HAM CASSEROLE AU GRATIN

Ham and eggs are combined with a cheese sauce in this tasty casserole. Surprise a neighbor home from the hospital with it

1 c. elbow macaroni	1 c. cubed cooked ham
¾ c. chopped celery	(½″)
½ c. chopped onion	4 hard-cooked eggs,
½ c. butter or regular	chopped
margarine	½ c. soft bread crumbs
1 (10½ oz.) can condensed	¼ c. chopped pimientos
cream of chicken soup	½ c. saltine cracker crumbs
1½ c. milk	1 tblsp. melted butter or
1½ c. shredded Cheddar	regular margarine
cheese	

Cook macaroni in boiling salted water in Dutch oven until almost tender. Drain. Rinse with cold water. Drain well.

Sauté celery and onion in ½ c. melted butter in 3-qt. saucepan until tender (do not brown). Add soup. Gradually stir in milk. Slowly add cheese, stirring constantly, until melted. Remove from heat. Add ham, eggs, bread crumbs and pimientos;

mix well. Turn into greased 11×7×1½" baking dish. Combine cracker crumbs and 1 tblsp. melted butter. Sprinkle on top.

Bake in 350° oven 30 minutes or until hot and bubbly. Makes 6 servings.

NOODLE/BEEF CASSEROLE

This protein-rich casserole features cottage ·cheese, sour cream and Cheddar cheese. It's like lasagna but easier to make

2½ c. medium noodles
1½ lbs. ground beef
1 c. chopped onion
1 tsp. salt
1½ tsp. oregano leaves
1 tsp. basil leaves
1 (1 lb.) can stewed
　tomatoes
2 (8 oz.) cans tomato sauce

1 (8 oz.) carton creamed
　cottage cheese (small or
　large curd)
¼ c. dairy sour cream
½ c. minced green pepper
¼ c. minced green onions
1 c. shredded Cheddar
　cheese

Cook noodles in boiling salted water in Dutch oven until almost tender. Drain. Rinse with cold water. Drain well.

Cook ground beef, onion, salt, oregano and basil in 12" skillet until well browned. Remove excess fat. Add stewed tomatoes and tomato sauce. Remove from heat. Add cooked noodles; mix well.

Combine cottage cheese, sour cream, green pepper and green onions in bowl; mix well. Place ½ of meat mixture in 3-qt. casserole. Top with cottage cheese mixture. Cover with remaining meat mixture. Sprinkle with Cheddar cheese.

Bake in 375° oven 45 minutes or until hot and bubbly. Makes 8 servings.

HAM JAMBALAYA CASSEROLE

An unusual rice dish featuring ham, shrimp and mushrooms

2 c. diced cooked ham	1 (4 oz.) can sliced
1 c. chopped onion	mushrooms
½ c. chopped green pepper	¼ c. slivered blanched
½ c. chopped celery	almonds
2 tblsp. cooking oil	3 tblsp. minced fresh parsley
2 chicken bouillon cubes	¾ c. uncooked regular rice
1 c. boiling water	½ lb. small shrimp, cooked,
1 (1 lb.) can tomatoes, cut	or 1 (8 oz.) can cooked
up	shrimp, drained

Sauté ham, onion, green pepper and celery in hot oil in 12″ skillet until tender (do not brown). Dissolve bouillon cubes in boiling water. Add bouillon mixture, tomatoes, undrained mushrooms, almonds, parsley and rice. Bring mixture to a boil. Pour into 2-qt. casserole. Cover.

Bake in 400° oven 30 minutes. Uncover. Stir in shrimp. Bake 5 more minutes. Makes 6 to 8 servings.

SAUSAGE NOODLE HOT DISH

Regular pork sausage links can be substituted for the Italian sweet sausage if you wish

8 oz. fine noodles	2 (8 oz.) cans tomato sauce
1 lb. Italian sweet pork	½ tsp. Worcestershire sauce
sausage	½ tsp. salt
½ c. chopped green pepper	½ tsp. oregano leaves
½ c. chopped onion	⅛ tsp. pepper
2 (1 lb.) cans tomatoes,	1 bay leaf
cut up	Grated Parmesan cheese

Cook noodles in boiling salted water in Dutch oven until almost tender. Drain. Rinse with cold water. Drain well.

Remove casing from pork sausage. Break pork sausage into chunks and cook in Dutch oven until it begins to change color. Add green pepper and onion. Sauté until mixture is well browned. Pour off excess fat. Add tomatoes, tomato sauce, Worcestershire sauce, salt, oregano, pepper and bay leaf. Bring mixture to a boil. Add drained noodles; mix well. Turn into 13×9×2″ baking dish. Cover with aluminum foil.

Bake in 350° oven 25 minutes. Remove foil. Sprinkle with Parmesan cheese before serving. Makes 6 servings.

BEEF AND STUFFING SQUARES

Just add a vegetable and a green salad for a complete meal

2 c. chopped celery and leaves
1 c. chopped onion
¼ c. butter or regular margarine
8 c. soft bread cubes (¼″)
1 lb. ground beef
¼ c. chopped fresh parsley
1 (10½ oz.) can condensed beef bouillon or broth
2 eggs
2 tsp. rubbed sage
¼ tsp. pepper
½ c. milk
Easy Mushroom Gravy (recipe follows)

Sauté celery and onion in melted butter in 10″ skillet until tender (do not brown).

Combine sautéed vegetables, bread cubes, ground beef, parsley, beef bouillon, eggs, sage, pepper and milk in large bowl. Mix lightly, but well. Press ground beef mixture into greased 11×7×1½″ baking dish.

Bake in 350° oven 40 minutes or until top is golden brown. Cut into 8 squares. Serve topped with Easy Mushroom Gravy. Makes 8 servings.

Easy Mushroom Gravy: Combine 1½ c. beef broth, 1 (4 oz.)

can sliced mushrooms, drained, 2 tsp. Worcestershire sauce and ¼ tsp. browning for gravy in saucepan. Bring to a boil. Combine 3 tblsp. cornstarch and 3 tblsp. water in jar. Cover and shake to blend. Gradually stir into boiling liquid. Boil 1 minute. Makes about 2 cups.

PASTRY-TOPPED PORK PIE

This meat pie was a favorite in our Countryside Test Kitchens

Pastry for 1-crust 9″ pie	¼ tsp. ground ginger
1/16 tsp. thyme leaves	⅛ tsp. dry mustard
¼ c. chopped onion	1½ c. chicken broth
1 c. chopped green pepper	½ tsp. browning for gravy
3 tblsp. butter or regular	3 c. cubed cooked pork
margarine	3 c. sliced pared carrots,
3 tblsp. flour	cooked and drained
1 tsp. salt	

Prepare pastry, adding thyme to mixture. Set aside.

Sauté onion and green pepper in melted butter in 10″ skillet until tender (do not brown). Add flour, salt, ginger and dry mustard; cook 1 minute, stirring constantly. Gradually stir in chicken broth. Cook over medium heat, stirring constantly, until mixture thickens. Add browning for gravy; stir well. Stir in pork and carrots. Pour mixture into 11×7×1½″ baking dish.

Roll out pastry to fit top of dish. Place over filling; seal edges. Cut vents.

Bake in 400° oven 35 minutes or until golden brown. Let stand 5 minutes before serving. Makes 6 servings.

CELERY SEED DRESSING

Tangy sweet and sour salad dressing to serve on tossed greens

1 c. salad oil	1 tsp. celery seeds
¼ c. light corn syrup	1 tsp. salt
¼ c. vinegar	1 tsp. dry mustard
1 tblsp. grated onion	1 tsp. paprika

Combine all ingredients in jar. Cover tightly and shake well. Chill thoroughly. Shake well before serving over tossed salad greens. Makes 2 cups.

MIXED VEGETABLE DRESSING

Attractive dressing with bright-colored bits of vegetables

1 c. salad oil	¼ c. chopped onion
⅓ c. vinegar	¼ c. chopped celery
1 tblsp. sugar	¼ c. chopped green pepper
2 tsp. salt	¼ c. chopped pared carrots
½ tsp. celery seeds	2 tblsp. diced pimientos
¼ tsp. pepper	

Combine oil, vinegar, sugar, salt, celery seeds and pepper in jar. Cover tightly and shake well. Add onion, celery, green pepper, carrots and pimientos. Chill thoroughly. Shake well before serving over tossed salad greens. Makes about 2 cups.

AN AFTERNOON SURPRISE FOR THE CONVALESCENT

"Just thought I'd drop by with these homemade rolls and see how you're feeling." That's a familiar phrase in a farm community and most welcomed by convalescents when it's midafternoon and they're feeling a bit let down.

We have some mouth-watering rolls and homemade jam that are just the perfect little thought to present to an ailing friend. You will make a big hit if you bake and take the American Apple Pie. It's stuffed with apples and has just the right amount of spices. Or fill a basket with homemade Brown Sugar Refrigerator Cookies and bring a thermos of hot cocoa for an extra surprise.

If you would like to make some new and exciting gift containers for these afternoon treats, turn to Chapter 9 for instructions. Consider making the whimsical mouse or elephant to fill with cookies and delight a child. If you're visiting a male friend, make the man with a top hat complete with sassy bow tie or the tissue paper owl.

Any of these containers filled with a tempting treat is guaranteed to lift anyone out of the doldrums.

ORANGE SWIRL BUNS .

Light airy rolls with refreshing orange filling and icing

2 pkgs. active dry yeast	2 eggs
2 c. lukewarm water	7¼ c. sifted flour
(110–115°)	½ c. soft butter or regular
½ c. sugar	margarine
½ c. butter or regular	1½ c. sugar
margarine	1 tblsp. grated orange rind
⅔ c. nonfat dry milk	Thin Orange Icing (recipe
2 tsp. salt	follows)

Sprinkle yeast on lukewarm water in mixing bowl; stir to dissolve. Add ½ c. sugar, ½ c. butter, dry milk, salt, eggs and 2 c. flour. Beat with electric mixer at medium speed until smooth, about 2 minutes, scraping bowl occasionally. Or beat with spoon until batter is smooth.

Gradually stir in enough remaining flour to make a soft dough that leaves the sides of the bowl. Turn out on floured surface and knead until smooth and satiny, about 10 minutes.

Place dough in greased bowl; turn over to grease top. Cover and let rise in a warm place until doubled, about 1½ hours.

Combine ½ c. butter, 1½ c. sugar and orange rind in bowl; mix well. Set aside.

Divide dough in half. Roll out half into 14×7" rectangle. Sprinkle with ½ of sugar mixture. Roll up like jelly roll from long side. Cut into 12 slices. Place in greased 13×9×2" baking pan. Repeat with remaining dough. Let rise until doubled, about 45 minutes.

Bake in 350° oven 25 minutes or until golden brown. Remove from pans; cool on racks. While still warm, glaze with Thin Orange Icing. Makes 24 rolls.

Thin Orange Icing: Combine 2½ c. sifted confectioners sugar and 3 tblsp. orange juice in small bowl; beat until smooth.

GOLDEN YEAST ROLLS

Our recipe tester said these rolls are super delicious

½ c. butter or regular margarine	2 pkgs. active dry yeast
⅓ c. sugar	½ c. lukewarm water (110°)
1½ tsp. salt	4½ c. sifted flour
2 tblsp. instant potato flakes	Melted butter or regular margarine
1 c. hot water	

Combine butter, sugar, salt, potato flakes and 1 c. hot water in mixing bowl. Cool to lukewarm.

Sprinkle yeast on ½ c. lukewarm water; stir to dissolve. Add yeast mixture and 1 c. flour to butter mixture. Beat with electric mixer at medium speed until smooth, about 2 minutes, scraping bowl occasionally. Or beat with spoon until batter is smooth.

Gradually add enough remaining flour to make a soft dough that leaves the sides of the bowl. DO NOT KNEAD. Place dough in greased bowl; grease top with oil. Cover and let rise in a warm place until doubled, about 1¼ hours.

Turn dough onto floured surface. Divide dough in half. Shape one half into 12 balls with floured hands. Place in greased 8" square baking pan. Repeat with remaining dough. Let rise until doubled, about 45 minutes.

Bake in 375° oven 20 minutes or until golden brown. Remove from pans; cool on racks. While still warm, brush with melted butter. Makes 24 rolls.

CHERRY APRICOT JAM

"I received this tangy apricot jam as a Christmas gift. I now share many jars of it with my friends," says a Michigan woman

2 (1 lb.) boxes dried apricots, cut up	2 (1 lb. 4 oz.) cans crushed pineapple
4 c. water	1 c. cut-up red maraschino cherries
4 c. sugar	

Place apricots in bowl. Add 4 c. water. Let stand overnight.

Combine apricots and liquid, sugar and undrained pineapple in Dutch oven. Bring mixture to a boil; reduce heat. Simmer, uncovered, 30 minutes or until almost thick. Add cherries. Cook 1 more minute.

Immediately ladle into 13 hot, sterilized half-pint jars. Adjust lids. Cool on wire racks 12 to 24 hours. Check jars for airtight seals. Makes 13 half-pints.

AMERICAN APPLE PIE

An excellently spiced apple pie with a superb flaky crust

3 c. sifted flour	⅔ c. sugar
1 tblsp. confectioners sugar	2 tblsp. flour
1 tsp. salt	1 tsp. ground cinnamon
1¼ c. lard	¼ tsp. ground nutmeg
Milk	¼ tsp. salt
1 egg, beaten	1 tblsp. lemon juice
6 c. thinly sliced, pared tart apples	2 tblsp. butter or regular margarine

Sift together 3 c. flour, confectioners sugar and 1 tsp. salt into bowl. Cut in lard with pastry blender or two knives until mixture resembles fine crumbs. Add enough milk to beaten egg to make ½ c. liquid. Add egg mixture to crumb mixture; toss with fork to make a soft dough. Divide dough almost in half. Roll larger portion to about ⅛" thickness on floured surface. Line 9" pie plate with pastry.

Combine apples, sugar, 2 tblsp. flour, cinnamon, nutmeg, ¼ tsp. salt and lemon juice in bowl; toss to coat apples. Arrange ½ of apple mixture in lined pie plate. Dot with butter. Top with remaining apples.

Roll out remaining dough to fit top of pie. Adjust top crust and flute edge; cut vents.

Bake in 400° oven 55 minutes or until apples are tender. Cool on rack. Makes 6 to 8 servings.

BROWN SUGAR REFRIGERATOR COOKIES

An heirloom recipe for generations in one Wisconsin family

2 c. brown sugar, firmly packed	1 tsp. vanilla
	3½ c. sifted flour
1 c. melted butter or regular margarine	1 tsp. baking soda
	1 c. chopped pecans
2 eggs	

Beat together brown sugar and butter in mixing bowl until well blended, using electric mixer at medium speed. Add eggs, one at a time, beating well after each addition. Beat in vanilla.

Sift together flour and baking soda. Stir into creamed mixture. Then stir in pecans. Cover bowl with aluminum foil and refrigerate 1 hour.

Shape dough into 2 (12") rolls, about 1½" in diameter. Wrap in plastic wrap. Refrigerate overnight.

Cut rolls in ¼" thick slices. Place slices, about 2" apart, on greased baking sheets.

Bake in 375° oven 10 to 12 minutes or until golden brown. Remove from baking sheets; cool on racks. Makes about 8 dozen.

TAKE A TOUCH OF SUNSHINE TO A SICK CHILD

An Ohio farm wife with children of her own knows just what will appeal to a cranky youngster who longs to be outdoors instead of confined to bed. She makes up batches of her homemade pudding mix and pours the dry powder into a small plastic bag, ties it and puts it into an empty tin can covered with bright shiny wrapping paper. Next she wraps a big bundle of crayons with colored tissue paper. When she visits the youngster, she takes the mix labeled with the child's name along with a note telling the child to use the can to hold the new crayons after the pudding is gone.

We have borrowed several ideas from farm women who give homemade mixes as gifts. These mixes are especially appealing to youngsters of all ages.

For example, teen-agers love chili and spaghetti. One farm wife made up her chili and spaghetti mix into sauces. She sent a spaghetti dinner to the delighted teen-ager. And, along with it, a shoe box filled with individual packets of the dry mix so that her mother could make it again. "Wow, what a neat gift," was the response.

Another homemade mix treat that any youngster will love—a big jar filled with Country-style Granola. It can be eaten as a "munchie" or a cereal, or used in a recipe for cookies or apple crisp. Tie the recipes onto the jar with a big bow so that Mother can make them later.

PUDDING MIX

Creamy pudding every time with this easy-to-use mix

2¾ c. nonfat dry milk	¾ c. cornstarch
1½ c. sugar	1 tsp. salt

Combine all ingredients in bowl; stir until well blended. Store in tightly covered container in a cool place. Makes 5 cups.

Directions to pack with mix: Store Pudding Mix in a cool place and use to make Vanilla Pudding (recipe follows).

VANILLA PUDDING

1¼ c. Pudding Mix	1 egg, slightly beaten
2½ c. milk or water	1½ tsp. vanilla
1 tblsp. butter or regular margarine	

Combine Pudding Mix and milk in heavy 2-qt. saucepan. Cook over medium heat, stirring constantly, until thickened. Add butter and remove from heat.

Stir some of hot mixture into egg. Blend egg into pudding; cook 1 minute. Remove from heat. Add vanilla. Pour into dessert glasses. Serve warm or chilled. Makes 6 servings.

CHOCOLATE PUDDING MIX

A protein-rich dessert for the convalescing child

5 c. nonfat dry milk	¾ c. baking cocoa
1½ c. sugar	1 tsp. salt
1¼ c. unsifted flour	

Combine all ingredients in bowl; stir until thoroughly blended. Store in covered container in a cool place. Makes 5 cups.

Directions to pack with mix: Store Chocolate Pudding Mix in a cool place and use to make Chocolate Pudding (recipe follows).

CHOCOLATE PUDDING

1¼ c. Chocolate Pudding Mix	1 tblsp. butter or regular margarine
1 egg, beaten	¾ tsp. vanilla
2½ c. water	

Place Chocolate Pudding Mix in saucepan.

Combine egg and water and stir into mix. Cook, stirring constantly, until mixture thickens and is smooth. Remove from heat. Add butter and vanilla. Pour into dessert glasses. Serve warm or chilled. Makes 6 servings.

COUNTRY-STYLE GRANOLA

When your hospitalized neighbor feels better, give a container of granola to him. Perfect as cereal or as a snack

5 c. old-fashioned rolled oats	½ c. brown sugar, firmly packed
1½ c. wheat germ	½ c. cooking oil
1 c. shredded coconut	⅓ c. water
1 c. chopped peanuts	2 tsp. vanilla
½ c. whole bran cereal (not flakes)	

Combine oats, wheat germ, coconut, peanuts, bran cereal and brown sugar in large bowl; mix well. Combine oil, water and vanilla; pour over cereal mixture. Mix thoroughly. Turn mixture into 15½ × 10½ × 1" jelly roll pan or shallow roasting pan.

Bake in 350° oven 1 hour, stirring every 15 minutes. Cool and store in covered containers. Makes about 10 cups.

Directions to pack with granola: Serve Country-style Granola as a ready-to-eat cereal or a snack or use to make Granola Cookies or Granola/Apple Crisp (recipes follow).

GRANOLA COOKIES

½ c. butter or regular margarine	¾ c. sifted flour
½ c. brown sugar, firmly packed	½ tsp. baking soda
½ c. sugar	½ tsp. salt
1 egg	2 c. Country-style Granola
1 tsp. vanilla	1 (6 oz.) pkg. semi-sweet chocolate pieces

Cream together butter, brown sugar and sugar in bowl until light and fluffy, using electric mixer at medium speed. Beat in egg and vanilla.

Sift together flour, baking soda and salt. Stir into creamed mixture. Add Country-style Granola and chocolate pieces; mix well. Drop mixture by teaspoonfuls, about 2″ apart, on greased baking sheets.

Bake in 350° oven 10 to 12 minutes or until lightly browned. Remove from baking sheets; cool on racks. Makes about 4 dozen.

GRANOLA/APPLE CRISP

4 c. sliced pared apples
¼ tsp. ground cinnamon
1½ c. Country-style Granola
⅔ c. brown sugar, firmly
    packed

⅓ c. unsifted flour
⅓ c. melted butter or
    regular margarine

Place apples in greased 8″ square baking pan. Sprinkle with cinnamon.

Combine Country-style Granola, brown sugar and flour in bowl; mix well. Stir in melted butter. Sprinkle mixture over apples.

Bake in 350° oven 35 minutes or until apples are tender and topping is golden brown. Serve warm. Makes 6 servings.

SLOPPY JOE SEASONING MIX

A change of diet for a teen-ager recovering from a broken leg. Surprise the skier with Sloppy Joe Burgers

1 tblsp. instant minced
    onion
1 tsp. green pepper flakes
1 tsp. salt
1 tsp. cornstarch

½ tsp. sugar
½ tsp. instant minced garlic
¼ tsp. dry mustard
¼ tsp. celery seeds
¼ tsp. chili powder

Combine all ingredients. Place on 6" square of aluminum foil and seal with drugstore wrap. Repeat recipe to make as many packages as desired. Makes 1 package.

Directions to pack with seasoning: Store in a cool place. Use Sloppy Joe Seasoning Mix to make Sloppy Joe Burgers and New Orleans Franks (recipes follow).

SLOPPY JOE BURGERS

1 lb. ground beef	1 (6 oz.) can tomato paste
1 pkg. Sloppy Joe Seasoning Mix	1¼ c. water
	6 hamburger buns

Brown ground beef in skillet; drain off excess fat. Blend in Sloppy Joe Mix. Stir in tomato paste and water. Cover and simmer over low heat 10 minutes. Serve hot between split buns. Makes 6 sandwiches.

NEW ORLEANS FRANKS

1 c. uncooked regular rice	1 pkg. Sloppy Joe Seasoning Mix
1 lb. frankfurters	1 (15 oz.) can kidney beans, drained and rinsed
1 tblsp. salad oil	
1 (6 oz.) can tomato paste	
1¼ c. water	

Cook rice as directed on package.

Meanwhile, cut each frankfurter in fourths crosswise; brown in hot oil in skillet. Stir in tomato paste, water and Sloppy Joe Seasoning Mix. Add kidney beans. Bring to a boil; reduce heat, cover and simmer 10 minutes. Serve over cooked rice. Makes 6 servings.

SPAGHETTI SAUCE MIX

This versatile seasoning mix makes any spaghetti sauce better

1 tblsp. instant minced onion	1½ tsp. salt
1 tblsp. parsley flakes	½ tsp. instant minced garlic
1 tblsp. cornstarch	1 tsp. sugar
2 tsp. green pepper flakes	¾ tsp. Italian seasoning

Combine all ingredients. Place on 6″ square of aluminum foil and seal with drugstore wrap. Repeat recipe to make as many packages as desired. Makes 1 package.

Directions to pack with mix: Store in a cool place. Use Spaghetti Sauce Mix to make Noodles with Meat Sauce or Spaghetti with Meat Sauce (recipes follow).

NOODLES WITH MEAT SAUCE

1 lb. ground beef	12 oz. medium noodles (about 9 c. uncooked)
1 pkg. Spaghetti Sauce Mix	2 c. grated process sharp American cheese
1 (6 oz.) can tomato paste	
2 c. water	

Cook ground beef in large skillet until browned. Drain off excess fat. Stir in Spaghetti Sauce Mix, tomato paste and water. Bring to a boil. Reduce heat, cover; cook 20 minutes.

Meanwhile, cook noodles by package directions; drain well. Add American cheese to meat mixture; stir until cheese is melted. Stir in noodles. Makes 6 servings.

SPAGHETTI WITH MEAT SAUCE

1 lb. ground beef	2 c. water
1 pkg. Spaghetti Sauce Mix	12 oz. spaghetti
1 (6 oz.) can tomato paste	Grated Parmesan cheese

Brown ground beef in skillet. Drain off excess fat. Stir in Spaghetti Sauce Mix, tomato paste and water; bring to a boil. Reduce heat; cover and simmer 20 minutes.

Meanwhile, cook spaghetti by package directions; drain well. Serve spaghetti topped with meat sauce. Sprinkle with Parmesan cheese. Makes 6 servings.

CHILI SEASONING MIX

"I took a serving of Ranch-style Chili to a teen-ager recovering from an accident. It was a real hit," a Missouri woman says

3 tblsp. flour	½ tsp. ground cumin
2 tblsp. instant minced onion	½ tsp. crushed dried red pepper
1½ tsp. chili powder	½ tsp. instant minced garlic
1 tsp. salt	½ tsp. sugar

Combine all ingredients. Place on 6″ square of aluminum foil and seal with drugstore wrap. Repeat recipe to make as many packages as desired. Makes 1 package.

Directions to pack with seasoning: Store in a cool place. Use Chili Seasoning Mix to make Ranch-style Chili or Texas Meatball Stew (recipes follow).

RANCH-STYLE CHILI

1 lb. ground beef	½ c. water
1 pkg. Chili Seasoning Mix	1 (15 oz.) can kidney beans
1 (1 lb.) can tomatoes, cut up	

Brown ground beef in skillet. Drain off excess fat. Blend in Chili Seasoning Mix, tomatoes, water and beans. Bring mixture to a boil; reduce heat. Cover and simmer 10 minutes. Makes 4 to 6 servings.

TEXAS MEATBALL STEW

1 lb. ground beef	1 (1 lb.) can tomatoes, cut
1 egg, beaten	up
¼ c. dry bread crumbs	1 (15 oz.) can kidney beans
2 tblsp. milk	1 c. elbow macaroni
½ tsp. salt	1 pkg. Chili Seasoning Mix
1 tblsp. cooking oil	2 c. water

Thoroughly mix together ground beef, egg, bread crumbs, milk and salt. Form into 1" balls. Brown meatballs on all sides in hot oil in Dutch oven. Pour off excess fat.

Add tomatoes, kidney beans, uncooked macaroni, Chili Seasoning Mix and water; bring to a boil, stirring gently. Reduce heat and simmer about 15 minutes, stirring occasionally. Makes 6 servings.

MEAT LOAF SEASONING MIX

This mix adds both flavor and moistness to a basic meat loaf

2 c. dry bread crumbs	1 tsp. pepper
½ c. nonfat dry milk	¼ c. instant minced onion
2 tblsp. salt	¼ c. parsley flakes
4 tsp. poultry seasoning	

Combine all ingredients in bowl. Mix thoroughly. Store in tightly covered container in a cool place. Stir to mix thoroughly before measuring to use. Makes 3 cups.

Directions to pack with mix: Store in a cool place. Use Meat Loaf Seasoning Mix as a seasoning in your favorite meatball recipe or make Tasty Beef Loaf (recipe follows).

TASTY BEEF LOAF

½ c. water   1½ lbs. ground beef
1 egg, beaten
¾ c. Meat Loaf Seasoning
  Mix

Blend together water, egg and Meat Loaf Seasoning Mix in bowl. Let stand 2 minutes. Thoroughly mix in ground beef. Shape into 8×4″ loaf in shallow baking pan.

Bake in 350° oven 1 hour 15 minutes. Makes 6 servings.

Chapter 3

MADE WITH LOVE FOR YOUR BIRTHDAY

There are so many ways to say happy birthday with a homemade treasure from your kitchen. Sometimes it's just a "wee" thought for a friend or neighbor to let her know you are thinking of her on that special day. Or it might be a gorgeous birthday cake that is time-consuming to make, but worth the effort.

Among farm homemakers, a very popular way to say "happy your-day" is to cook a complete meal featuring favorite dishes of the birthday person. These range from something as simple as meat loaf to chicken in a fancy sauce.

A wonderful way to remember the elderly person who lives alone is to fix homemade individual "TV dinners" using all the foods he or she likes the very best. A thoughtful Illinois farmer's wife has been fixing "personalized" TV birthday dinners for several years for an elderly friend. She brings a big bouquet of flowers from her garden along with the birthday feast. "It's wonderful to see her face light up with a happy smile. I don't know who enjoys it the most—me or the birthday celebrant."

BEAUTIFUL BIRTHDAY CAKES

"Every year when I ask my husband or my son what cake they would like me to bake for their birthday, the answer is always the same—anything as long as it's chocolate," a dairy farmer's wife from Iowa wrote us.

As we separated cake recipes sent to us from good farm cooks, it was evident that chocolate cake ranks highest in birthday requests.

And so, for all the chocolate fans around the country, we have some outstanding deep, dark, delicious cakes. A high, tender-crumbed Cream-filled Chocolate Cake is the favorite birthday cake of all five members of an Ohio family. "Try it, you'll love it," wrote a Nebraska birthday cake baker when she sent us her Quick Chocolate Cake recipe. We tried it and our staff demolished the entire cake in less than fifteen minutes! Chocolate Angel Food, sent to us from a Texas ranch, is a 100-year-old heirloom recipe that originated in Germany. All this feather-light cake needs is a dusting of confectioners sugar before you set the candles aglow.

Whenever one North Dakota woman gives a birthday cake to a neighbor or friend, she puts it on an inexpensive glass plate. She attaches a note suggesting that perhaps the birthday recipient might like to use the plate when giving a cake as a gift. Many of her gift plates have made the "rounds" in her community and returned to her kitchen. Then she recycles them again. "Everyone loves the idea," she told us.

DEVIL'S FOOD CAKE

Fine-textured layer cake with creamy chocolate frosting that was a big hit when tested in our Countryside Test Kitchens

2 c. sifted flour	⅔ c. shortening
1¾ c. sugar	1 c. water
1¾ tsp. baking soda	1 tsp. vanilla
1 tsp. salt	3 eggs
¼ tsp. baking powder	Cocoa Frosting (recipe
⅔ c. baking cocoa	follows)

Sift together flour, sugar, baking soda, salt, baking powder and cocoa into mixing bowl. Add shortening, water and vanilla. Beat with electric mixer at medium speed 2 minutes, scraping bowl occasionally.

Add eggs; beat 3 more minutes. Pour batter into 2 greased and floured 9″ round cake pans.

Bake in 350° oven 35 minutes or until cakes test done. Cool in pans on racks 10 minutes. Remove from pans; cool on racks.

Spread top of one layer with Cocoa Frosting. Place other layer on top. Frost sides and top of cake with remaining frosting. Makes 12 servings.

Cocoa Frosting: Combine 1 (1 lb.) box confectioners sugar, 4 tblsp. baking cocoa, 1 tblsp. shortening, 1 beaten egg, 1 tsp. vanilla and 3 tblsp. light cream or milk in bowl. Beat with electric mixer at medium speed until smooth and creamy.

QUICK CHOCOLATE CAKE

The secret for this cake's success is its delightful frosting

1¾ c. sifted cake flour	½ c. butter or regular
1¼ c. sugar	margarine
½ c. baking cocoa	2 eggs
1 tsp. baking powder	1 tsp. vanilla
1 tsp. salt	Creamy Fudge Frosting
½ tsp. baking soda	(recipe follows)
1 c. milk	

Sift together cake flour, sugar, cocoa, baking powder, salt and baking soda into large bowl. Add milk and butter. Beat with electric mixer at medium speed 2 minutes. Add eggs and vanilla; beat 2 more minutes at medium speed. Pour batter into 2 greased and waxed paper-lined 8″ round cake pans.

Bake in 350° oven 30 to 35 minutes or until cakes test done.

Cool in pans on racks 10 minutes. Remove from pans; cool on racks.

Spread top of one layer with Creamy Fudge Frosting. Place other layer on top. Frost sides and top of cake with remaining frosting. Makes 12 servings.

Creamy Fudge Frosting: Combine 3 c. sifted confectioners sugar, 1 slightly beaten egg, ½ c. soft butter or regular margarine and 4 (1 oz.) squares unsweetened chocolate, melted, and 1 tsp. vanilla in bowl. Beat with electric mixer at high speed until smooth and creamy.

CREAM-FILLED CHOCOLATE CAKE

Elegant cake with excellent fudgy chocolate flavor. Sure to look lovely aglow with colorful birthday candles

3 c. sifted cake flour
1½ tsp. baking soda
¾ tsp. salt
¾ c. butter or regular
  margarine
2¼ c. sugar
3 eggs
1½ tsp. vanilla
3 (1 oz.) squares
  unsweetened chocolate,
  melted

1½ c. iced water
Fluffy Cream Filling (recipe
  follows)
Chocolate Cream Frosting
  (recipe follows)
Chopped walnuts

Sift together cake flour, baking soda and salt.

Cream together butter and sugar in mixing bowl until light and fluffy, using electric mixer at medium speed. Add eggs, one at a time, beating well after each addition. Blend in vanilla and chocolate.

Add dry ingredients alternately with iced water, beating well after each addition. Pour batter into 3 greased and waxed paper-lined 9″ round cake pans.

Bake in 350° oven 30 minutes or until cakes test done. Cool in pans on racks 10 minutes. Remove from pans; cool on racks.

Spread top of one layer with ½ of Fluffy Cream Filling. Top with second cake layer. Spread with remaining Fluffy Cream Filling. Top with third layer. Spread sides and top of cake with Chocolate Cream Frosting. Decorate top of cake with chopped walnuts. Makes 12 servings.

Fluffy Cream Filling: Combine 2⅓ c. sifted confectioners sugar, ½ c. shortening, dash of salt, 3 tblsp. milk and ½ tsp. vanilla in bowl. Beat with electric mixer at medium speed until light and creamy.

Chocolate Cream Frosting: Cream together 1 (3 oz.) pkg. cream cheese, softened, and 2 tblsp. milk in mixing bowl, using electric mixer at high speed. Blend in 2½ c. sifted confectioners sugar, 2 (1 oz.) squares unsweetened chocolate, melted, and ½ tsp. vanilla. Beat with electric mixer until smooth, adding a little more milk if necessary.

CHOCOLATE ANGEL FOOD

"So good that it melts in your mouth," one tester commented

4 tblsp. baking cocoa	1½ c. egg whites (12)
1 c. sugar	1 tsp. cream of tartar
¾ c. sifted cake flour	¼ tsp. salt
½ c. sugar	1 tsp. vanilla

Sift together cocoa and 1 c. sugar.

Sift together cake flour and ½ c. sugar.

Beat egg whites, cream of tartar and salt in mixing bowl until foamy, using electric mixer at high speed. Add cocoa mixture, 1 tblsp. at a time, beating at high speed until stiff, glossy peaks form. Blend in vanilla.

Add flour mixture in 4 parts, folding about 15 strokes after each addition. Spoon batter into ungreased 10″ tube pan. Pull metal spatula through batter once to break large air bubbles.

Bake in 325° oven 1 hour or until cake tests done. Invert tube pan on funnel or bottle to cool. When completely cooled, remove from pan. Makes 12 servings.

FROSTED VELVET LAYER CAKE

Lemon-scented yellow cake layers swirled with fluffy icing

2½ c. sifted cake flour	1 tsp. lemon flavoring
1⅔ c. sugar	½ tsp. vanilla
4 tsp. baking powder	5 egg yolks
1 tsp. salt	Fluffy White Frosting
½ c. shortening	(recipe follows)
1¼ c. milk	

Sift together cake flour, sugar, baking powder and salt into mixing bowl. Add shortening and half of milk. Beat with electric mixer at medium speed 2 minutes, scraping bowl occasionally. Add remaining milk, lemon flavoring, vanilla and egg yolks. Beat with electric mixer 2 more minutes. Pour batter into 2 greased and floured 9″ round cake pans.

Bake in 350° oven 30 minutes or until cakes test done. Cool in pans on racks 10 minutes. Remove from pans; cool on racks.

Spread top of one layer with Fluffy White Frosting. Place second layer on top. Frost sides and top of cake with frosting. Makes 12 servings.

Fluffy White Frosting: Combine 2 egg whites, 1½ c. sugar, ⅓ c. water, 2 tsp. light corn syrup and dash of salt in top of double boiler. Beat 1 minute with electric mixer at high speed. Place over simmering water and cook, beating constantly, until mixture forms stiff peaks, about 7 minutes. Remove from heat. Transfer to mixing bowl. Add 1 tsp. vanilla. Beat until mixture is of spreading consistency.

BOHEMIAN POPPY SEED CAKE

Popular with those who do not care for extra-sweet desserts

½ c. poppy seeds
1 c. milk
2½ c. sifted flour
2½ tsp. baking powder
¾ c. butter or regular
  margarine

1½ c. sugar
1½ tsp. vanilla
4 egg whites, stiffly beaten
Custard Filling (recipe
  follows)

Soak poppy seeds in milk in small bowl 2 hours.

Sift together flour and baking powder.

Cream together butter and sugar in mixing bowl until light and fluffy, using electric mixer at medium speed. Beat in vanilla.

Add dry ingredients alternately with poppy seed mixture, beating well after each addition. Fold in egg whites. Pour batter into 2 greased and floured 9″ round baking pans.

Bake in 350° oven 25 minutes or until cakes test done. Cool in pans on racks 5 minutes. Remove from pans; cool on racks.

Cut each layer in half horizontally. Fill layers with Custard Filling. Place fourth layer on top. Swirl top of cake with remaining filling. Store in refrigerator until serving time. Makes 12 servings.

Custard Filling: Combine ¾ c. sugar and 2 tblsp. cornstarch in 2-qt. saucepan; mix well. Gradually stir in 2 c. milk. Cook over medium heat, stirring constantly, until mixture thickens. Add a little of hot mixture to 4 well-beaten egg yolks; stir well. Add yolk mixture to hot custard. Cook over low heat 1 minute, stirring constantly. Remove from heat. Stir in 2 tblsp. butter or regular margarine, 3 drops yellow food color and 2 tsp. vanilla. Cool well.

SWEET BIRTHDAY THOUGHTS

Candies and cookies are especially welcome gifts to give to family members away from home. "When a package from Oregon arrives on my birthday morning," a Michigan woman wrote us, "I know it is going to be filled with Mother's English Toffee —loaded with almonds. Each piece is wrapped separately with loving care."

The Peanut Brittle Deluxe recipe sent to us from a farm wife in Pennsylvania is just like its name—deluxe. This thrifty woman saves her coffee cans because she makes lots of brittle to give as gifts. She covers the cans with wallpaper remnants and ties them with bag string (recycled from the barn) instead of ribbon.

Peanut butter fans will love to receive a batch of Peanut Fudge, Peanut Butter Bars or Peanut Butter Sandwich Cookies. Why not splurge and give an assortment using some of each?

If you are giving to a birthday youngster, pile cookies into one of the animals featured in Chapter 9. The half-pint mouse or the owl bag would delight any child and they are both fun to make.

ENGLISH TOFFEE

An Oregon homemaker substitutes filberts for almonds

2 c. butter or regular margarine
2 c. sugar
2 tblsp. light corn syrup
6 tblsp. water
1 c. slivered blanched almonds
1 (6 oz.) pkg. semi-sweet chocolate pieces
2 tblsp. shortening
3/4 c. toasted sliced almonds

Melt butter in heavy 10″ skillet. Add sugar, corn syrup, water and 1 c. almonds. Cook over medium heat, stirring constantly, until mixture boils. Continue cooking, stirring occasionally, until mixture reaches soft crack stage (290°) on candy thermometer. Pour mixture onto greased 17×14″ baking sheet.

Melt chocolate pieces with shortening over hot water; stir until smooth. Spread on toffee. Sprinkle with ¾ c. almonds. When chocolate is set, break toffee into pieces. Store in cool place. Makes 3 lbs.

PEANUT BRITTLE DELUXE

For gift-giving, pack this candy in decorated coffee cans and top with plastic lids. Will keep fresh for several weeks

2 c. sugar	4 tblsp. butter or regular
1 c. light corn syrup	margarine
¼ c. water	2 tsp. baking soda
1½ c. salted peanuts	1 tsp. vanilla

Combine sugar, corn syrup and water in heavy 3-qt. saucepan. Cook over medium heat, stirring constantly, until sugar is dissolved. Continue cooking, stirring occasionally, until mixture reaches soft crack stage (285°) on candy thermometer. Add peanuts and butter. Cook, stirring constantly, to hard crack stage (300°) on candy thermometer. Remove from heat. Rapidly stir in baking soda and vanilla. (Mixture will foam up.)

Turn mixture onto 2 greased baking sheets. Spread out with metal spatula as thin as possible. When candy begins to set, loosen from baking sheets. Turn brittle over, then stretch and pull brittle as thin as possible using two forks. When completely cooled, break into pieces. Makes about 2 lbs.

PEANUT FUDGE

"It has become a tradition to send this fudge to my son in college for his birthday," a Wisconsin mother wrote us

⅔ c. milk
2 tblsp. light corn syrup
2 c. sugar
2 (1 oz.) squares
    unsweetened chocolate,
    cut up

2 tblsp. butter or regular
    margarine
1 tsp. vanilla
1 c. finely chopped, roasted
    salted peanuts

Combine milk, corn syrup, sugar and chocolate in heavy 2-qt. saucepan. Cook over medium heat, stirring constantly, until sugar is dissolved. Continue cooking over medium heat until candy reaches soft ball stage (236°) on candy thermometer. Stir occasionally to prevent sticking.

Remove from heat; add butter. Cool to 110° without stirring.

Add vanilla. Beat until fudge begins to lose its shine. Stir in peanuts. Quickly pour into greased 8″ square baking pan. Cut in squares when candy is completely cooled. Makes 1½ lbs.

PEANUT BUTTER BARS

Rich, moist bar cookies sure to please peanut butter lovers

½ c. butter or regular
    margarine
½ c. brown sugar, firmly
    packed
½ c. sugar
1 egg
1 tsp. vanilla
⅓ c. crunch-style peanut
    butter

1 c. sifted flour
½ tsp. baking soda
¼ tsp. salt
1 c. quick-cooking oats
1 c. semi-sweet chocolate
    pieces
Vanilla Glaze (recipe
    follows)

Cream together butter, brown sugar and sugar in mixing bowl until light and fluffy, using electric mixer at medium speed. Beat in egg and vanilla. Blend in peanut butter.

Sift together flour, baking soda and salt. Stir dry ingredients into creamed mixture; blend well. Stir in oats.

Spread mixture in greased 13×9×2" baking pan. Sprinkle with chocolate pieces.

Bake in 350° oven 25 minutes or until done. Cool in pan on rack. While still warm, drizzle with Vanilla Glaze. When cooled, cut in 48 (2×1½") bars. Makes 48 bars.

Vanilla Glaze: Combine ½ c. sifted confectioners sugar, ¼ c. peanut butter, 2 tblsp. butter or regular margarine, ¼ c. hot milk and ½ tsp. vanilla in bowl. Beat with electric mixer at high speed until smooth.

PEANUT BUTTER SANDWICH COOKIES

Surprise your children with these double peanut butter-flavored cookies filled with a special creamy filling

1 c. butter or regular
  margarine
1 c. sugar
1 c. brown sugar, firmly
  packed
2 eggs
1 c. crunch-style peanut
  butter

1 tsp. vanilla
3 c. sifted flour
2 tsp. baking soda
¼ tsp. salt
Peanut Butter Filling
(recipe follows)

Cream together butter, sugar and brown sugar in mixing bowl until light and fluffy, using electric mixer at medium speed. Add eggs, one at a time, beating well after each addition. Beat in peanut butter and vanilla.

Sift together flour, baking soda and salt. Stir into creamed mixture. Form mixture into 1" balls. Place about 2" apart on greased baking sheets. Press with floured fork, making crisscross pattern on each.

Bake in 375° oven 8 minutes or until golden brown. Remove from baking sheets; cool on racks. When completely cooled, spread one cookie with Peanut Butter Filling. Place another cookie on top, forming sandwich cookies. Makes 3½ dozen sandwich cookies.

Peanut Butter Filling: Combine ½ c. crunch-style peanut butter, 3 c. sifted confectioners sugar, 4 tblsp. milk and 1 tsp. vanilla in bowl. Beat with electric mixer at medium speed until smooth and creamy.

GRATED CHOCOLATE MERINGUES

Crinkled-topped meringue cookies with a mild chocolate flavor

½ c. shortening	¼ tsp. salt
2 c. sugar	2 (1 oz.) squares semi-sweet
3 eggs	chocolate, grated
2 tsp. vanilla	Sugar
2½ c. sifted flour	Whole blanched almonds
2 tsp. baking powder	

Cream together shortening and sugar in mixing bowl until light and fluffy, using electric mixer at medium speed. Add eggs, one at a time, beating well after each addition. Beat in vanilla.

Sift together flour, baking powder and salt. Stir into creamed mixture. Stir in chocolate. Drop mixture by teaspoonfuls, about 2″ apart, on greased baking sheets. Flatten with a drinking glass dipped in sugar. Place almond in center of each.

Bake in 350° oven 12 minutes or until done. Remove from baking sheets; cool on racks. Makes about 4½ dozen.

CINNAMON CANDIED WALNUTS

Substitute pecans for walnuts for a change of pace

2½ c. walnut halves   1 tsp. ground cinnamon
1 c. sugar   ½ tsp. salt
½ c. water   1 tsp. vanilla

Place walnuts on 15½ ×10½ ×1″ jelly roll pan. Heat in 375°
oven 5 minutes, stirring once. Turn off oven, but do not remove
walnuts.

Combine sugar, water, cinnamon and salt in buttered heavy
2-qt. saucepan. Cook over medium heat, stirring constantly,
until sugar dissolves and mixture boils. Cook until mixture
reaches soft ball stage (236°) on candy thermometer, without
stirring. Remove from heat.

Beat mixture with wooden spoon 1 minute or until it begins to
get creamy. Add vanilla and warm walnuts; stir until walnuts are
coated. Turn out on buttered baking sheet. Separate at once into
small clusters, using two forks. Makes about 1 lb.

PECAN CARAMEL CLUSTERS

An Illinois woman has made these "pecan turtles" for years

1 c. light cream   ½ tsp. vanilla
1 c. sugar   2½ c. chopped pecans
½ c. light corn syrup   1 (6 oz.) pkg. semi-sweet
¼ tsp. salt   chocolate pieces
3 tblsp. butter or regular
   margarine

Heat light cream in heavy 2-qt. saucepan to lukewarm
(110°). Reserve ½ c. cream; set aside.

Add sugar, corn syrup and salt to remaining ½ c. cream in
saucepan. Cook over medium heat, stirring constantly, until

mixture boils. Slowly stir in ½ c. reserved cream. Cook, stirring constantly, 5 minutes.

Stir in butter, 1 tsp. at a time, stirring constantly. Cook over low heat, stirring constantly, until mixture reaches soft ball stage (234°) on candy thermometer. Remove from heat. Stir in vanilla. Cool 3 minutes.

Arrange pecans on waxed paper-lined baking sheet. Drop mixture by teaspoonfuls onto pecans. As clusters cool, remove with metal spatula to another waxed paper-lined baking sheet. Push remaining pecans together and drop the rest of the mixture. If mixture becomes too thick, heat over low heat.

Melt chocolate pieces over hot water; stir until smooth. Spread on top of pecan clusters. Let stand until chocolate is set. Store candies in cool place. Makes about 4 dozen.

SPECIAL BIRTHDAY REQUESTS

Surprise a birthday celebrator with a main dish or even a complete meal as your gift. A Nebraska woman remembers her older shut-in friends with a special birthday dinner all portioned out on a recycled aluminum TV dinner tray. You can even make a decorative cardboard back for the tray and write your own birthday message on it to add a festive touch. Or perhaps you might like to make a hand-crafted floral gift tag to attach to the main dish. Turn to Chapter 9 for directions on how to make these easy decorations.

We have picked six recipes that are top birthday requests and teamed them into three birthday menus. These are all farmers' favorites and, in each case, they chose pie for dessert!

The Oriental Meatballs are very special to an Iowa farmer and he looks forward to his daughter-in-law fixing them every year for "his" day. Meat Loaf Wellington is fancy indeed. "Best I've ever eaten" is the comment of a North Dakota man.

BIRTHDAY MENU

GROUND BEEF ROLL*

BUTTERED CORN   SLICED TOMATOES

LUSCIOUS LIME PIE*

*Recipes follow

GROUND BEEF ROLL

An extra-special flavor combination for the meat loaf lover

1 c. finely chopped celery	½ c. soft bread crumbs
½ c. chopped onion	¼ c. minced onion
¼ c. melted butter or regular margarine	2 tblsp. chopped fresh parsley
1 (4 oz.) can sliced mushrooms	1 tsp. salt
3 c. soft bread cubes (¼″)	¼ tsp. pepper
2 tsp. poultry seasoning	2 eggs, slightly beaten
2 lbs. ground beef	Onion Gravy (recipe follows)

Sauté celery and ½ c. onion in melted butter in small skillet until tender (do not brown).

Drain mushrooms; reserve ⅓ c. liquid. Combine bread cubes, poultry seasoning, sautéed vegetables, mushrooms and ⅓ c. reserved liquid in bowl. Mix lightly, but well. Set aside.

Combine ground beef, bread crumbs, ¼ c. onion, parsley, salt, pepper and eggs in bowl. Mix lightly, but well. Pat mixture into 9″ square on heavy-duty aluminum foil. Top with stuffing mixture. Roll up like jelly roll, using foil to aid in shaping loaf. Wrap up in aluminum foil, placing seam side of meat loaf down. Place on rack in shallow roasting pan.

Bake in 375° oven 1 hour. Open foil. Bake 15 more minutes

or until loaf is nicely browned. Serve with Onion Gravy. Makes
6 to 8 servings.

Onion Gravy: Sauté 1 medium onion, thinly sliced, in 4 tblsp.
melted butter in 2-qt. saucepan until tender (do not brown).
Stir in 4 tblsp. flour. Gradually stir in 1 (13¾ oz.) can beef
broth. Add ¼ tsp. Worcestershire sauce, ½ tsp. browning for
gravy and dash of pepper. Cook over medium heat, stirring constantly, until mixture comes to a boil. Serve over meat roll.

LUSCIOUS LIME PIE

*This bright lime-green pie is especially good topped with dollops
of sweetened whipped cream and thin lime slices*

1⅓ c. graham cracker crumbs	1 (14 oz.) can sweetened condensed milk
¼ c. sugar	½ c. fresh lime juice
¼ c. melted butter or regular margarine	1 tsp. grated lime rind
1 env. unflavored gelatin	10 drops green food color
¾ c. cold water	4 drops yellow food color

Combine graham cracker crumbs, sugar and butter in bowl;
mix well. Press crumb mixture into 9" pie plate.

Bake in 375° oven 7 minutes or until golden brown. Cool on
rack.

Soften gelatin in cold water in small saucepan. Stir over low
heat until gelatin is dissolved.

Combine gelatin, sweetened condensed milk, lime juice, lime
rind, green and yellow food color in bowl; mix well. Pour into
graham cracker crust. Chill in refrigerator until set. Makes 6 to
8 servings.

BIRTHDAY MENU

BAKED CHICKEN BREASTS WITH ALMOND SAUCE*
GREEN BEANS   CRANBERRY SAUCE
FAKE PECAN PIE*

* Recipes follow

BAKED CHICKEN BREASTS WITH ALMOND SAUCE

"My guests always ask for the recipe," a Kentucky woman said

1 clove garlic, minced
¼ c. butter or regular
   margarine
1 tblsp. paprika
1 tblsp. lemon juice
¼ tsp. salt
4 whole chicken breasts,
   split
1 (10¾ oz.) can condensed
   cream of mushroom soup

¼ c. milk
1 (4 oz.) can mushroom
   stems and pieces, drained
½ tsp. Worcestershire sauce
½ c. dairy sour cream
½ c. toasted slivered
   almonds
2 tblsp. flour
¼ c. water

Sauté garlic in melted butter in small skillet until tender (do not drain). Remove from heat. Add paprika, lemon juice and salt. Coat chicken breasts on all sides in butter mixture. Place chicken, skin side up, in 13×9×2" baking dish.

Bake in 350° oven 30 minutes.

Meanwhile, combine soup, milk, mushrooms, Worcestershire sauce and sour cream in bowl. Mix well. Spoon mixture over chicken. Sprinkle with almonds. Return to oven. Bake 30 more minutes or until chicken is tender. Remove chicken; place on serving platter. Keep warm.

Pour drippings into 2-qt. saucepan. Combine flour and water; blend well. Stir into drippings. Cook over medium heat, stirring constantly, until mixture thickens. Pour over chicken. Makes 6 servings.

FAKE PECAN PIE

If you like pecan pie, you will enjoy a wedge of this

¾ c. crunchy nutlike cereal nuggets	3 tblsp. melted butter or regular margarine
½ c. warm water	1 tsp. vanilla
3 eggs	⅛ tsp. salt
¾ c. sugar	1 unbaked 9″ pie shell
1 c. dark corn syrup	

Combine cereal and warm water in bowl. Let stand until water is absorbed.

Combine eggs and sugar in bowl. Beat with electric mixer at medium speed until well blended. Beat in corn syrup, butter, vanilla and salt; blend well. Stir in cereal mixture. Pour mixture into pie shell.

Bake in 350° oven 50 minutes or until top of pie is puffy. Cool on rack. Serve with puffs of sweetened whipped cream if you wish. Makes 6 to 8 servings.

BIRTHDAY MENU

POTATO-FROSTED MEAT LOAF*
CARROTS   APPLESAUCE
ALL-AMERICAN LEMON MERINGUE PIE*

* Recipes follow

POTATO-FROSTED MEAT LOAF

"Meat and potatoes" men will rave about this moist beef loaf

2 lbs. ground beef	2 lbs. potatoes, pared and
2 c. soft bread crumbs	quartered (6 medium)
½ c. finely chopped onion	¼ c. melted butter or
2 tblsp. minced fresh parsley	regular margarine
2 tsp. marjoram leaves	⅓ c. hot milk
2 tsp. salt	1 egg, well beaten
¼ tsp. pepper	1 c. shredded Cheddar
2 eggs, slightly beaten	cheese
1 c. tomato juice	

Combine ground beef, bread crumbs, onion, parsley, marjoram, salt, pepper, 2 eggs and tomato juice in bowl. Mix lightly, but well. Shape into 9" loaf on greased 15½×10½×1" jelly roll pan.

Bake in 350° oven 50 minutes.

Meanwhile, cook potatoes in boiling salted water 25 minutes or until tender. Drain well. Mash potatoes with vegetable masher.

Beat in butter and milk. Stir in 1 egg. Spread meat loaf with hot potato mixture. Then sprinkle with Cheddar cheese. Place in broiler, 9" from source of heat, until cheese melts and surface is lightly browned. Let stand 5 minutes before slicing. Makes 6 to 8 servings.

ALL-AMERICAN LEMON MERINGUE PIE

If your husband prefers pie for his birthday, try this one

½ c. sugar
5 tblsp. cornstarch
¼ tsp. salt
1½ c. boiling water
3 eggs, separated
½ c. sugar

⅓ c. lemon juice
1½ tblsp. grated lemon rind
1 tblsp. butter or regular
    margarine
1 baked 9″ pie shell
6 tblsp. sugar

Combine ½ c. sugar, cornstarch and salt in top of a double boiler; mix well. Gradually stir in boiling water. Cook over boiling water, stirring constantly, until mixture is thick enough to mound slightly when dropped from a spoon. Cover and cook 10 minutes, stirring occasionally.

Beat egg yolks slightly in small bowl. Stir in ½ c. sugar. Stir a little hot mixture into egg yolks; blend well. Gradually stir all of egg yolk mixture into cooked custard; blend well. Cook 2 minutes, stirring constantly. Remove from heat. Add lemon juice, lemon rind and butter. Cool 5 minutes. Pour into baked pie shell.

Beat egg whites in bowl until foamy, using electric mixer at high speed. Gradually add 6 tblsp. sugar, 1 tblsp. at a time, beating well after each addition. Continue beating until stiff peaks form. Spoon meringue over pie filling, spreading evenly to edge of pie shell, sealing all around.

Bake in 425° oven 5 minutes or until meringue is lightly browned. Cool on rack. Makes 6 to 8 servings.

ORIENTAL MEATBALLS

A Washington homemaker freezes the uncooked meatballs ahead. ahead. So handy to serve for dinner to unexpected company

1½ lbs. ground beef
1½ c. soft bread crumbs
2 tblsp. chopped onion
2 tblsp. chopped fresh
   parsley
1 tsp. salt
½ tsp. celery salt
¼ tsp. pepper
¼ tsp. dry mustard
1 egg, slightly beaten
⅓ c. milk
2 tblsp. cooking oil
1 (1 lb. 4 oz.) can pineapple
   chunks

1 (4 oz.) can mushroom
   stems and pieces, drained
2 medium tomatoes, cut in
   wedges
1 medium green pepper, cut
   in strips
½ c. brown sugar, firmly
   packed
2 tblsp. cornstarch
½ tsp. ground ginger
½ tsp. salt
½ c. cider vinegar
2 tblsp. soy sauce
Fluffy hot rice

Combine ground beef, bread crumbs, onion, parsley, 1 tsp. salt, celery salt, pepper, mustard, egg and milk in bowl. Mix lightly, but well. Shape mixture into 18 meatballs. Brown meatballs on all sides in hot oil in 12″ skillet. Remove meatballs as they brown. Pour off excess fat.

Drain pineapple, reserving 1 c. liquid. Combine meatballs, pineapple, mushrooms, tomatoes and green pepper in skillet. Set aside.

Combine brown sugar, cornstarch, ginger and ½ tsp. salt in 2-qt. saucepan. Gradually stir in 1 c. reserved liquid, vinegar and soy sauce. Cook over medium heat, stirring constantly, until mixture comes to a boil. Remove from heat. Pour over meatball mixture. Place over medium heat; heat thoroughly. Serve over rice. Makes 6 servings.

MEAT LOAF WELLINGTON

"I must have this recipe," one taster remarked after only one bite
of this meat loaf. *"I'm having company tomorrow"*

1½ lbs. ground beef	¼ tsp. pepper
¾ c. soft bread crumbs	2 eggs, slightly beaten
½ c. shredded carrots	1 (10 oz.) pkg. pie crust mix
⅓ c. chopped onion	or pastry for 2-crust 9″ pie
¼ c. ketchup	1 egg yolk, slightly beaten
2 tblsp. milk	1 tblsp. water
1 tblsp. Worcestershire	Mushroom Onion Sauce
sauce	(recipe follows)
1 tsp. salt	

Combine ground beef, bread crumbs, carrots, onion, ketchup,
milk, Worcestershire sauce, salt, pepper and eggs in bowl. Mix
lightly, but well. Shape meat mixture into 7×4″ loaf on
15½×10½×1″ jelly roll pan.

Bake in 350° oven 50 minutes or until meat loaf is done.
Remove from oven; cool in pan on rack 25 minutes.

Meanwhile, prepare pie crust mix according to package directions or prepare your favorite pastry for 2-crust 9″ pie. Remove
⅓ of dough. Roll out on lightly floured surface to 9×6″ rectangle. Place on baking sheet. Place cooled meat loaf on dough.
Roll out remaining ⅔ of dough to 12×9″ rectangle. Place over
meat loaf. Trim edges to 1″. Seal and flute edges. Prick dough
with fork making air vents. Mix together egg yolk and water in
small bowl. Brush over surface of dough.

Bake in 400° oven 20 minutes or until golden brown. Cut in
slices and serve with Mushroom Onion Sauce. Makes 6 servings.

Mushroom Onion Sauce: Combine 1 (10½ oz.) can condensed
cream of onion soup and ½ c. milk in 2-qt. saucepan; blend
well. Add 1 (4 oz.) can mushroom stems and pieces, drained.
Cook, stirring constantly, until mixture comes to a boil. Stir in 2
tblsp. chopped fresh parsley.

Chapter 4

FOODS TO COMFORT FRIENDS AND NEIGHBORS

When there's a death in the family or any other severe emotional stress that calls for neighborly care, farm homemakers are quick to respond with comforting gifts of food. Many women wrote to tell us that often the entire community pitches in and contributes homemade food to feed out-of-town relatives who have come to attend a funeral. Sometimes the church groups organize preparation of the food that will be needed to serve over one hundred people and each person is asked to contribute a specific dish. "In that way," as one Kansas woman explained, "you don't end up with fifty people bringing hot rolls while only ten have brought a hot main dish or salad."

No matter whether it is an assigned dish or a personal gesture, each woman brings what she considers a favorite. It's usually a dish that is easy to serve.

Casseroles are a natural and so are salads and hot homemade rolls with quick serve-in-the-pan cakes for dessert.

We feature a medley of recipes that have been used over and over again and have been much appreciated during times of bereavement.

They are homey and comforting foods. In fact, you can combine several of these recipes and produce a meal to take to a bereaved family after all the guests have left . . . the time when they most need a little loving care and good food to give them a lift.

SALADS AND ROLLS

"I always offer to bring the homemade rolls and a salad when there has been a death in the family. Everyone likes them and they go so well with all the hot dishes," confided a Minnesota woman.

Often the recipes for salad are doubled or tripled and some women bring three different salads that go well with baked ham or roast beef.

Tangy Marinated Cabbage Slaw is a perfect choice. If there is any left over, it keeps beautifully in the refrigerator for up to two weeks.

German-style Potato Salad and the creamy Tuna Macaroni Salad go well with any meat.

MARINATED CABBAGE SLAW

An Alabama homemaker has proudly served this salad for years. Her mother brought the recipe here from the old country

12 c. shredded cabbage
1½ c. chopped onion
¾ c. sugar
1 tsp. salt
1 tblsp. prepared yellow
   mustard

½ tsp. celery seeds
1 c. white vinegar
½ c. salad oil

Combine cabbage, onion and sugar in large bowl; toss lightly.
Combine salt, mustard, celery seeds and vinegar in 2-qt. saucepan. Cook over medium heat, stirring occasionally, until mixture comes to a boil. Add oil; bring back to a boil. Pour hot dressing over cabbage mixture. DO NOT STIR. Cover with plastic wrap. Let marinate 24 hours in refrigerator before serv-

ing. (Salad can be stored up to 2 weeks in refrigerator.) Toss
before serving. Makes 20 servings.

GERMAN-STYLE POTATO SALAD

Sweet and sour sauce enhances this salad. If prepared in advance, store in refrigerator and warm slightly before serving

8 strips bacon, diced	5 c. sliced, cooked potatoes
2 tblsp. sugar	(about 2 lbs.)
1 tblsp. flour	3 hard-cooked eggs, sliced
1 tsp. dry mustard	1 c. chopped onion
1 tsp. salt	2 tblsp. chopped fresh
⅓ c. vinegar	parsley
⅔ c. water	

Fry bacon in 10″ skillet until crisp. Add sugar, flour, mustard,
salt, vinegar and water. Cook over medium heat, stirring constantly, until mixture thickens. Remove from heat.

Combine potatoes, eggs, onion and parsley in large bowl.
Pour hot sauce over potato mixture; toss gently to mix. Serve
warm. Makes 6 servings.

TUNA MACARONI SALAD

This unusual salad is always a favorite at buffet luncheons

8 oz. elbow macaroni	1 large tomato, cut up
1 (7 oz.) can solid pack	¼ tsp. pepper
tuna, drained	1½ c. salad dressing or
½ c. chopped onion	mayonnaise
½ c. chopped celery	1 tblsp. sugar
4 hard-cooked eggs,	3 tblsp. milk
chopped	3 tblsp. lemon juice
½ c. sliced pimiento-stuffed	1 tsp. prepared mustard
olives	1 tsp. salt

Cook macaroni in boiling salted water in Dutch oven until tender. Drain. Rinse with cold water. Drain well.

Combine macaroni, tuna, onion, celery, eggs, olives, tomato and pepper in large mixing bowl.

Combine salad dressing and sugar in bowl. Gradually stir in milk and lemon juice; blend well. Add mustard and salt; blend well. Pour over macaroni mixture; toss gently to mix. Cover with plastic wrap. Refrigerate until thoroughly chilled. Makes 8 servings.

MIXED VEGETABLE MARINADE

Colorful, crisp vegetable salad that can be made up quickly and then stored for up to 5 days in the refrigerator

1 medium cauliflower, cut up

4 medium carrots, pared and cut in 2″ strips

1 (1 lb.) can wax beans, drained

1 (1 lb.) can whole green beans, drained

1 c. sliced celery

1 medium onion, sliced

1 (8 oz.) bottle regular Italian salad dressing

12 medium pitted ripe olives

Cook cauliflower and carrots in boiling salted water in Dutch oven 5 minutes or until tender-crisp. Drain. Plunge into iced water; drain well.

Combine cooled vegetables, wax beans, green beans, celery, onion, salad dressing and olives in bowl. Toss gently to mix. Cover; refrigerate overnight. Salad can be stored up to 5 days. Makes 10 servings.

FARM HOUSE ROLLS

Giant super-light yeast rolls that are sure to please a crowd

1 c. milk, scalded	¼ c. lukewarm water
¼ c. sugar	(110°)
1 tsp. salt	1 egg
¼ c. shortening	3½ c. sifted flour
1 pkg. active dry yeast	

Combine milk, sugar, salt and shortening in mixing bowl. Cool to lukewarm.

Sprinkle yeast over lukewarm water; stir to dissolve.

Add yeast mixture, egg and 1 c. flour to milk mixture. Beat with electric mixer at medium speed, about 2 minutes, scraping bowl occasionally. Or beat with spoon until batter is smooth.

Gradually stir in remaining flour. Dough is soft. DO NOT KNEAD. Place dough in lightly greased bowl; grease top with oil. Cover and let rise in warm place until doubled, about 2 hours.

Punch down dough. Shape into 15 balls with well-floured hands. Place in greased 13×9×2″ baking pan. Cover and let rise until doubled, about 45 minutes.

Bake in 400° oven 10 to 12 minutes or until golden brown. Delicious served warm or cold. Makes 15 rolls.

NO-KNEAD CRESCENT ROLLS

This dough can be made ahead and refrigerated up to one week. When you need fresh rolls, just shape and bake them

1 c. milk, scalded	2 pkgs. active dry yeast
½ c. butter or regular	½ c. lukewarm water
margarine	(110°)
½ c. sugar	6 c. sifted flour
1 tblsp. salt	4 eggs

Combine milk, butter, sugar and salt in mixing bowl. Cool to lukewarm.

Sprinkle yeast over lukewarm water; stir to dissolve.

Add yeast mixture and 2 c. flour to milk mixture. Beat with electric mixer at medium speed, about 2 minutes, scraping bowl occasionally. Add eggs; beat 2 more minutes at medium speed. Stir in remaining flour. Dough will be sticky. Cover bowl with plastic wrap and then with aluminum foil. Let stand in refrigerator at least 2 hours. (Dough can be refrigerated for 1 week.)

Punch down dough. Divide in half. Roll into 14″ circle. Cut circle into 12 wedges. Roll up each wedge from wide end, forming a crescent. Place on greased baking sheets. Repeat with remaining dough. Cover and let rise in warm place until doubled, about 1½ hours.

Bake in 400° oven 8 to 10 minutes or until golden brown. Delicious served warm. Makes 24 rolls.

A SWEET TOUCH

Cookies and cakes that are quick to fix and can be frozen ahead are perfect to serve a crowd. A New York woman who helps to run a dairy farm with her husband believes in conserving time by baking two cakes at once. "Chocolate Chip Cake," she tells us, "is my stand-by cake to take when there is a death in the community." And she sent us a practical packaging tip: Place the frozen cake in a foil-lined shirt box so there is no need for the recipient to wash and return the pan.

All the cakes are moist and flavorful and keep well. As for pies, apple pie is a popular choice. We present one from Kansas, Frosted Apple Raisin Pie, a bit unusual with its zingy orange frosting.

CHOCOLATE CHIP CAKE

A New York woman suggests packing this cake in a foil-lined shirt box so no baking pan or plate need be returned

2 c. sifted flour	2 tsp. vanilla
1 tsp. baking powder	1 c. dairy sour cream
1 tsp. baking soda	1 (6 oz.) pkg. semi-sweet
½ tsp. salt	chocolate pieces
½ c. butter or regular	½ c. chopped walnuts
margarine	¼ c. sugar
1 c. sugar	2 tblsp. baking cocoa
2 eggs	

Sift together flour, baking powder, baking soda and salt.

Cream together butter and 1 c. sugar in mixing bowl until light and fluffy, using electric mixer at medium speed. Add eggs, one at a time, beating well after each addition. Beat in vanilla.

Add dry ingredients alternately with sour cream to creamed mixture, beating well after each addition. Pour batter into greased 13×9×2″ baking pan. Combine chocolate pieces, walnuts, ¼ c. sugar and cocoa in small bowl; mix well. Sprinkle over cake batter.

Bake in 350° oven 35 minutes or until cake tests done. Cool in pan on rack. Makes 16 servings.

FROSTED APPLE RAISIN PIE

Luscious apple/raisin pie topped with tangy orange icing

6 c. sliced, pared tart apples	Pastry for 2-crust 9″ pie
¼ c. raisins	2 tblsp. orange juice
¼ c. sugar	3 tblsp. butter or regular
2 tblsp. flour	margarine
½ tsp. ground cinnamon	Orange Icing (recipe
⅛ tsp. salt	follows)

Combine apples, raisins, sugar, flour, cinnamon and salt in bowl; toss to coat apples. Arrange apple mixture in pastry-lined pie plate. Sprinkle with orange juice. Dot with butter. Adjust top crust and flute edge; cut vents.

Bake in 400° oven 40 minutes or until crust is golden and apples are tender. Cool on rack. While still warm, glaze top of pie with Orange Icing. Makes 6 to 8 servings.

Orange Icing: Combine 1 c. sifted confectioners sugar, 2 tblsp. orange juice and 1 tsp. grated orange rind in bowl; stir until smooth.

PEANUT/OAT BARS

Chewy bar cookies that are easy to prepare at the last minute

3½ c. quick-cooking oats
1 c. flaked coconut
⅔ c. butter or regular
  margarine
⅓ c. peanut butter
½ c. brown sugar, firmly
  packed

⅓ c. light corn syrup
¾ c. chopped salted
  peanuts
1 egg, beaten

Toast oats in shallow baking pan in 350° oven 8 minutes. Add coconut; toast 5 more minutes. Remove from oven.

Combine butter, peanut butter, brown sugar and corn syrup in 2-qt. saucepan; mix well. Cook over low heat until mixture is smooth. Remove from heat. Add to oat mixture, peanuts and egg in bowl; blend well. Press mixture firmly into well-greased 15½ × 10½ × 1″ jelly roll pan.

Bake in 350° oven 20 minutes or until golden brown. Cool in pan on rack. Cut into 48 (2½ × 1″) bars. Makes 48 bars.

GLAZED PINEAPPLE BARS

These rich moist bars were very popular with our testers

2¼ c. sifted flour
1½ c. sugar
1½ tsp. baking soda
½ tsp. salt
1 (20 oz.) can crushed
   pineapple

2 eggs
1 tsp. vanilla
1⅓ c. flaked coconut
½ c. chopped walnuts
Vanilla Glaze (recipe
   follows)

Sift together flour, sugar, baking soda and salt into mixing bowl. Add undrained pineapple, eggs and vanilla. Beat with electric mixer at medium speed about 2 minutes, scraping bowl occasionally. Pour batter into greased 15½×10½×1" jelly roll pan. Sprinkle with coconut and walnuts.

Bake in 350° oven 20 minutes or until bars test done. Cool in pan on rack. While still warm, pour Vanilla Glaze over bars. When cooled, cut in 36 (3½×1¼") bars. Makes 36 bars.

Vanilla Glaze: Combine ¾ c. sugar, ½ c. butter or regular margarine and ¼ c. evaporated milk in 2-qt. saucepan; mix well. Cook until mixture comes to a boil. Remove from heat.

CARROT/WALNUT BARS

This recipe makes two large pans of lightly spiced bars

2 c. sifted flour
2 c. sugar
2 tsp. baking soda
2 tsp. ground cinnamon
¼ tsp. salt
4 eggs

1 c. cooking oil
3 (4½ oz.) jars baby food
   strained carrots
½ c. chopped walnuts
Cream Cheese Frosting
   (recipe follows)

Sift together flour, sugar, baking soda, cinnamon and salt into mixing bowl. Add eggs, oil and carrots. Beat with electric mixer at medium speed 3 minutes, scraping bowl occasionally. Stir in walnuts. Pour mixture into 2 greased and floured 13×9×2″ baking pans.

Bake in 350° oven 30 minutes or until bars test done. Cool in pans on racks. Frost with Cream Cheese Frosting. Cut each pan into 32 (3×1″) bars. Makes 64 bars.

Cream Cheese Frosting: Combine 2 c. sifted confectioners sugar, 1 (8 oz.) pkg. softened cream cheese, ¼ c. soft butter or regular margarine and 1 tsp. vanilla in bowl. Beat with electric mixer at medium speed until light and fluffy.

DATE SNACK CAKE

Favorite family cake that stays moist for several days

1 c. boiling water	1 c. sugar
1 c. chopped dates	2 eggs
1¾ c. sifted flour	1 tsp. vanilla
2 tblsp. baking cocoa	1 (6 oz.) pkg. semi-sweet
1 tsp. baking soda	chocolate pieces
½ tsp. salt	1 c. chopped walnuts
1 c. butter or regular	Confectioners sugar
margarine	

Pour boiling water over dates in bowl. Let cool.

Sift together flour, cocoa, baking soda and salt.

Cream together butter and sugar in bowl until light and fluffy, using electric mixer at medium speed. Add eggs, one at a time, beating well after each addition. Beat in vanilla.

Add dry ingredients alternately with date mixture to creamed mixture, mixing well. Stir in chocolate pieces and walnuts. Pour batter into greased 13×9×2″ baking pan.

Bake in 325° oven 45 minutes or until cake tests done. Cool

in pan on rack. Dust with sifted confectioners sugar. Makes 16 servings.

BANANA CAKE SQUARES

Great out-of-hand cake squares with real banana flavor

2¼ c. sifted flour	2 eggs
2 tsp. baking powder	1⅓ c. mashed ripe bananas
1 tsp. baking soda	(3 large)
½ tsp. salt	1 tsp. vanilla
½ c. butter or regular	¼ c. milk
margarine	Confectioners sugar
1½ c. sugar	

Sift together flour, baking powder, baking soda and salt.

Cream together butter and sugar in mixing bowl until light and fluffy, using electric mixer at medium speed. Add eggs, one at a time, beating well after each addition. Blend in bananas and vanilla.

Add dry ingredients alternately with milk to creamed mixture, beating well after each addition. Pour batter into greased 13×9×2″ baking pan.

Bake in 350° oven 35 minutes or until cake tests done. Cool in pan on rack. Dust with confectioners sugar before serving. Makes 16 servings.

MOIST BANANA BREAD

"Best banana bread I've ever tasted," one tester remarked

2 c. sifted flour	1½ c. sugar
1 tsp. baking soda	2 eggs
¾ tsp. salt	1 c. mashed bananas
¾ c. butter or regular	1 tsp. vanilla
margarine	½ c. buttermilk

Sift together flour, baking soda and salt.

Cream together butter and sugar in mixing bowl until light and fluffy, using electric mixer at medium speed. Add eggs, one at a time, beating well after each addition. Blend in bananas and vanilla.

Add dry ingredients alternately with buttermilk to creamed mixture, beating well after each addition. Pour batter into greased and waxed paper-lined 9×5×3" loaf pan.

Bake in 325° oven 1 hour 15 minutes or until bread tests done. Cool in pan on rack 10 minutes. Remove from pan; cool on rack. Wrap loaf in aluminum foil and let stand 24 hours for easier slicing. Makes 1 loaf.

FROSTED CHOCOLATE SQUARES

Brownie-like squares with creamy rich chocolate frosting

1 c. butter or regular margarine	2 c. sifted flour
½ c. baking cocoa	1 tsp. baking soda
1 c. water	¾ tsp. salt
½ c. dairy sour cream	Chocolate Frosting (recipe follows)
2 c. sugar	¾ c. chopped pecans
2 eggs	

Combine butter, baking cocoa and water in 2-qt. saucepan; mix to blend. Cook over medium heat, stirring constantly, until mixture comes to a boil. Remove from heat; cool slightly.

Cream together sour cream, sugar and eggs in mixing bowl until well blended, using electric mixer at medium speed.

Sift together flour, baking soda and salt. Add dry ingredients alternately with cocoa mixture to creamed mixture, beating well after each addition. Pour batter into 2 greased 13×9×2" baking pans.

Bake in 350° oven 15 to 20 minutes or until done. Cool in pans on racks.

When cooled, frost with Chocolate Frosting. Sprinkle with pecans. Cut each pan into 24 squares. Makes 48.

Chocolate Frosting: Combine 2¼ c. sifted confectioners sugar, ¼ c. soft butter or regular margarine, 2 tblsp. baking cocoa and 3 tblsp. milk in bowl; beat until smooth.

MINIATURE CHEESECAKE JEWELS

Decorated cheesecakes that taste as good as they look

3 (8 oz.) pkgs. cream cheese, softened	5 eggs
1 c. sugar	1 pt. dairy sour cream
¼ tsp. salt	Assorted canned fruits
1 tsp. vanilla	Walnut halves or sliced almonds

Beat cream cheese in bowl with electric mixer at medium speed until smooth. Gradually beat in sugar. Blend in salt and vanilla. Add eggs, one at a time, beating well after each addition. Spoon mixture into paper-lined 1¼" muffin-pan cups, filling almost full.

Bake in 325° oven 30 minutes or until set. Cool in pans 5 minutes. Remove. When cool, cover and refrigerate. Can be stored up to 5 days.

Spread each cheesecake with sour cream. Decorate with cut-up fruits and nuts. Refrigerate. Makes 60.

Note: Undecorated cheesecakes can be frozen up to 1 month.

PEANUT/COCONUT PIE

A rich gooey pie which should please any pecan pie lover

2 eggs
¼ c. melted butter or
   regular margarine
½ c. sugar
1½ c. dark corn syrup
1 tsp. vanilla

½ c. chopped salted
   peanuts
½ c. flaked coconut
1 unbaked 9" pie shell with
   fluted edge

Combine eggs, butter and sugar in bowl. Beat with electric mixer at medium speed until well blended. Beat in corn syrup and vanilla; blend well. Stir in peanuts and coconut. Pour mixture into pie shell.

Bake in 400° oven 15 minutes. Reduce heat to 350° and bake 30 more minutes or until filling is set. Cool on rack. Makes 6 to 8 servings.

EASY-TO-FIX CASSEROLES

These casseroles feature everyday foods and they are great favorites with the men, many women have explained. Nothing fancy—just plain good eating, the kind of food we all want when we are under emotional stress.

If you are especially busy, choose one of the one-dish dinners that can be made ahead and refrigerated or frozen.

The Baked Chicken Scallop and the Cheese Macaroni Medley are often top choices to "run over to the neighbor just before supper time," as one farm woman put it. After the hectic days have subsided, it's so nice to remember your friends with a casserole and a basket of hot rolls.

BAKED CHICKEN SCALLOP

Complete meal-in-a-dish that is so simple to prepare

1 (3 lb.) broiler-fryer, cut up
1 tsp. salt
1 tsp. paprika
3 tblsp. cooking oil
4 c. sliced, pared potatoes

¾ c. chopped onion
1 (10¾ oz.) can condensed
    cream of mushroom soup
1 c. milk

Season broiler-fryer with salt and paprika. Brown chicken on all sides in hot oil in 10″ skillet. Remove chicken as it browns.

Place potatoes and onion in 11×7×1½″ baking dish. Combine soup and milk in saucepan; mix to blend. Heat, stirring constantly. Pour over potatoes and onions in baking dish. Top with chicken. Cover with aluminum foil.

Bake in 375° oven 45 minutes. Remove aluminum foil. Bake 30 more minutes or until potatoes and chicken are tender. Makes 4 servings.

CHEESE MACARONI MEDLEY

Hearty cheese-laced casserole that is rich in protein

1 c. elbow macaroni
1 lb. ground beef
½ tsp. salt
¼ tsp. pepper
1 c. chopped onion
1 c. green pepper strips
1 (4 oz.) can sliced
    mushrooms, drained
2 tblsp. butter or regular
    margarine

2 tblsp. flour
½ tsp. salt
2 c. milk
1 (10 oz.) pkg. Cheddar
    cheese, shredded (2½ c.)
1 (14½ oz.) can baby
    tomatoes, drained
½ c. shredded Cheddar
    cheese

Cook elbow macaroni in boiling salted water in Dutch oven until almost tender, about 15 minutes. Drain well.

Meanwhile, cook ground beef, ½ tsp. salt and pepper in 12″ skillet until meat begins to turn color. Add onion, green pepper and mushrooms. Continue to cook until mixture is well browned. Remove excess fat; set aside.

Melt butter in 2-qt. saucepan. Stir in flour and ½ tsp. salt. Cook 1 minute, stirring constantly. Gradually stir in milk. Cook until thickened. Remove from heat. Add 2½ c. Cheddar cheese, stirring until melted. Combine cheese sauce with meat mixture in skillet. Add macaroni; mix gently. Turn mixture into 11×7×1½″ baking dish. Top with tomatoes and ½ c. Cheddar cheese.

Bake in 350° oven 30 minutes or until hot. Makes 8 servings.

BEEF/CARROT CASSEROLE

Great combination of flavors in this nutritious hot dish

8 oz. medium noodles	¼ tsp. pepper
1 lb. ground beef	1 c. dairy sour cream
1 tblsp. butter or regular margarine	1 c. creamed large curd cottage cheese
¼ c. minced onion	¼ c. chopped fresh parsley
1 clove garlic, minced	1 c. sliced, cooked carrots
2 (8 oz.) cans tomato sauce	1 c. shredded Cheddar cheese
1 tsp. salt	

Cook noodles in boiling salted water in Dutch oven until almost tender. Drain. Rinse with cold water. Drain well.

Cook ground beef in melted butter in skillet. When meat begins to turn color, add onion and garlic. Sauté until meat is well browned. Stir in tomato sauce, salt and pepper. Simmer, uncovered, 5 minutes. Remove from heat.

Meanwhile, combine sour cream, cottage cheese, parsley and carrots in large bowl. Stir in cooked noodles.

Alternate layers of noodle mixture and meat mixture in greased 3-qt. casserole, beginning and ending with noodle mixture. Top with Cheddar cheese.

Bake in 350° oven 30 minutes or until hot. Makes 6 servings.

Note: Unbaked casserole can be frozen ahead. To heat: Bake, covered, in 400° oven 1 hour or until bubbly.

TWIN BEEF/NOODLE CASSEROLES

This recipe makes two casseroles . . . enough to serve a crowd

8 oz. medium noodles
1½ lbs. ground beef
½ lb. hot Italian pork
   sausage, cut in chunks
2 c. chopped green pepper
2 c. chopped onion
1 c. chopped celery
2 cloves garlic, minced
1 tsp. salt
1 (4 oz.) can sliced
   mushrooms
1 (10¾ oz.) can condensed
   tomato soup

1 (1 lb. 13 oz.) jar meatless
   spaghetti sauce
1 c. water
½ c. sliced, pitted ripe
   olives
1 tblsp. oregano leaves
1 tsp. basil leaves
1½ c. shredded Cheddar
   cheese
1 c. shredded mozzarella
   cheese

Cook noodles in boiling salted water in Dutch oven 4 minutes. Drain. Rinse with cold water. Drain well.

Cook ground beef and pork sausage in Dutch oven until it begins to turn color. Add green pepper, onion, celery, garlic and salt; cook until mixture is well browned. Stir in undrained mushrooms, tomato soup, spaghetti sauce, water, olives, oregano and basil. Bring mixture to a boil. Reduce heat and simmer 5 minutes. Combine beef mixture with noodles. Turn noodle mixture into 2 (2-qt.) casseroles. Top each with ½ of Cheddar cheese and ½ of mozzarella cheese. Cover.

Bake in 350° oven 25 minutes or until hot and bubbly. Makes 12 to 16 servings.

Note: Casseroles can be prepared ahead and refrigerated until baking time. Bake in 350° oven 1 hour or until hot and bubbly.

LATTICE CHEESE CASSEROLE

So good served with a tossed green salad and French bread

1½ lbs. ground beef
1¼ c. chopped onion
2 beef bouillon cubes
⅔ c. boiling water
1 (1 lb. 12 oz.) can
   tomatoes, cut up
1 (10½ oz.) can condensed
   cream of mushroom soup

1½ c. quick-cooking rice
⅛ tsp. oregano leaves
⅛ tsp. garlic powder
⅛ tsp. pepper
1 bay leaf
3 slices American process
   cheese, cut in ½" strips

Cook ground beef and onion in 10" skillet until well browned. Dissolve bouillon cubes in boiling water; set aside.

Add tomatoes, soup, rice, oregano, garlic powder, pepper and bay leaf to skillet. Stir in bouillon. Bring to a boil. Reduce heat and simmer 5 minutes or until rice is tender, stirring occasionally. Pour mixture into 2-qt. casserole. Remove bay leaf. Place cheese strips on top, crisscrossing in lattice fashion. Place under broiler just long enough to melt cheese. Makes 6 to 8 servings.

SUPER CHICKEN CASSEROLE

Hard-cooked eggs make this casserole different. So inexpensive to prepare and a complete meal-in-one-dish

1 (3 lb.) broiler-fryer, cut up	3 hard-cooked eggs,
4 c. water	chopped
1 c. chopped onion	1¼ c. milk
1 tsp. salt	1 (10¾ oz.) can condensed
¼ tsp. pepper	cream of mushroom soup
1 tsp. salt	¾ c. soft bread crumbs
2 c. medium noodles	2 tblsp. melted butter or
1 (8 oz.) can sliced	regular margarine
mushrooms	

Place broiler-fryer, water, onion, 1 tsp. salt and pepper in Dutch oven. Bring to a boil; reduce heat. Cover and simmer 1 hour or until chicken is tender. Remove chicken from broth. Reserve 2 c. of chicken broth. Cool chicken until it can be handled.

Remove chicken from bones; cut in chunks. Discard skin and bones. Set chicken aside.

Place reserved 2 c. chicken broth and 1 tsp. salt in 2-qt. saucepan. Heat broth to boiling. Add noodles and cook 4 minutes or until almost tender. (All the chicken broth will be absorbed.)

Drain mushrooms, reserving liquid. Place ½ of noodles in greased 13×9×2″ baking dish. Top with ½ of egg, then ½ of mushrooms and ½ of chicken. Repeat layers.

Gradually stir milk into soup in bowl; blend well. Stir in reserved mushroom liquid. Pour over chicken. Toss bread crumbs with butter. Sprinkle over top.

Bake in 350° oven 25 minutes or until hot. Makes 6 servings.

TWO BEAN/BEEF BAKE

Rib-sticking casserole that's perfect for a buffet supper

1 (10 oz.) pkg. frozen lima beans
1 lb. ground beef
½ c. chopped celery
½ c. chopped green pepper
½ c. chopped onion
1 (6 oz.) can tomato paste

2 (1 lb.) cans pork and beans in tomato sauce
1 c. water
1 tblsp. chili powder
½ tsp. salt
Tortilla chips

Cook lima beans in boiling salted water in 2-qt. saucepan until almost tender. Drain well.

Meanwhile, cook ground beef in 12″ skillet until meat begins to turn color. Add celery, green pepper and onion; cook until meat mixture is well browned. Stir in lima beans, tomato paste, pork and beans, water, chili powder and salt. Turn mixture into 2-qt. casserole.

Bake in 350° oven 30 minutes or until hot and bubbly. Garnish with tortilla chips before serving. Makes 8 servings.

Chapter 5

GIFTS THAT SAY "THANK YOU"

What do you give a neighbor who has done you a favor? Or what can you take as a gift for a host or hostess?

Farm women solve such problems in the best way of all. They give homemade food gifts that are very special—usually treasured recipes from their kitchens.

Gifts may change with the season. In the fall, a favorite gift is a sparkling jar of homemade jelly, pickles or preserves—the bounty of the rural homemaker's garden. In mid-January it's most likely to be a plump loaf of homemade bread or a fruited tea bread. During the hot summer months, homemade sauces to pour over heaping dishes of ice cream are popular—and most welcome—choices.

In addition to the homemade food gift, often an interesting but inexpensive container is given for storing or serving the food. A rancher's wife picks up small antique dishes and baskets whenever she goes to a garage sale to have on hand for gift giving. Many women save mayonnaise, pickle, peanut butter and olive jars year 'round. They preserve fruits and vegetables in standard canning jars during the summer. When a gift occasion arises, they spoon these homemade favorites into the jars they've saved and refrigerate. Decorated with gold seals, they make handsome gifts for little cost.

SOMETHING TO PLEASE YOUR HOSTESS

If you're tired of taking the usual box of candy or bunch of flowers as a hostess gift, borrow some of these different gift ideas that farm women have shared with us.

For example, any hostess would be delighted to receive a bottle of homemade wine vinegar. We give you three flavors to choose from—basil, tarragon and dill. And if it's a very special occasion, why not give all three vinegars nestled in a wicker basket? We have given a recipe to use with each vinegar. You might like to give the recipe along with the vinegar.

Is your hostess a gourmet cook? She might enjoy our specially blended Fines Herbs or Herb Salt to use in her recipes. Inexpensive salt shakers from the dime store would make excellent containers. Or give one of the cheese balls on a small wooden board to a hostess who likes to serve snacks before dinner.

Ice cream fanciers will welcome the homemade sauces to spoon over ice cream or to build a super sundae. For a fancier gift, give a pretty little pitcher along with a jar of homemade sauce.

BASIL WINE VINEGAR

Recycled steak sauce bottles make attractive containers for this vinegar. Tie each with a colorful bow

1 pt. dry white wine
1 pt. white vinegar
20 bunches fresh young basil

Place wine and vinegar in saucepan over low heat. Bring to scalding, but do not boil.

Meanwhile, wash basil and place in a sterilized quart jar. Pour hot liquid slowly over basil. Seal tightly and store in a dark place for 3 weeks. Strain vinegar through cheesecloth and pour into smaller sterilized bottles. Add a sprig of basil to each bottle if you wish. Makes 1 quart.

Directions to pack with vinegar: Use Basil Wine Vinegar as you would any other vinegar or use to make Consommé Madrilène (recipe follows).

CONSOMMÉ MADRILÈNE

2 (10½ oz.) cans condensed
    beef consommé
1 tsp. Basil Wine Vinegar

⅓ c. finely chopped celery
Lime slices

Combine consommé, Basil Wine Vinegar and celery; mix well. Refrigerate until firm.

Stir consommé before serving. Serve with thin lime slice on top of each serving. Makes 2½ cups.

TARRAGON WINE VINEGAR

Especially good in basic French-type salad dressings

1 pt. dry red wine
1 pt. cider vinegar
20 to 30 bunches fresh tarragon

Place wine and vinegar in saucepan over low heat. Bring to scalding, but do not boil.

Meanwhile, carefully wash tarragon and place in a sterilized quart jar. Slowly pour hot liquid over tarragon. Seal tightly and store in a dark place for 3 weeks. Strain vinegar through cheesecloth and pour into smaller sterilized bottles. Add a bunch of tarragon to each bottle if you wish. Makes 1 quart.

Directions to pack with vinegar: Use Tarragon Wine Vinegar as you would any other vinegar or use to make Oven-barbecued Chicken (recipe follows).

OVEN-BARBECUED CHICKEN

2 (2 lb.) broiler-fryers, split	2 tblsp. Tarragon Wine
1 c. tomato juice	Vinegar
1 c. chili sauce	1 tsp. chili powder
2 tsp. Worcestershire sauce	½ tsp. garlic salt

Lay chicken halves skin side up in shallow roasting pan. Bake in 400° oven 30 minutes.

Combine tomato juice, chili sauce, Worcestershire sauce, Tarragon Wine Vinegar, chili powder and garlic salt in bowl; blend well. Pour over chicken. Bake 30 minutes or until chicken is tender, basting frequently with sauce. Makes 8 servings.

DILL WINE VINEGAR

Pour this vinegar over a tossed tuna salad . . . so refreshing

**1 pt. dry white wine
1 pt. white vinegar
20 to 30 flowers of dill**

Place wine and vinegar in saucepan over low heat. Bring to scalding, but do not boil.

Meanwhile, wash dill and cut in 1″ lengths. Place in a sterilized quart jar. Pour hot liquid slowly over dill. Seal tightly and store in a dark place for 3 weeks. Strain vinegar through cheesecloth and pour into smaller sterilized bottles. Makes 1 quart.

Directions to pack with vinegar: Use Dill Wine Vinegar as you would any other vinegar or use to make Cabbage Australia (recipe follows).

CABBAGE AUSTRALIA

1 medium head cabbage   ½ c. Dill Wine Vinegar
2 c. water   4 tblsp. butter or regular
1 tsp. salt   margarine
1 tsp. sugar

Cut cabbage into 4 wedges and remove core.

Pour water into 2-qt. saucepan. Add salt, sugar and Dill Wine Vinegar. Bring to a boil and gently drop in cabbage wedges. Cook 15 minutes or just until cabbage is tender. Drain and serve, topping each wedge with 1 tblsp. butter. Makes 4 servings.

SALAD HERBS

A great blend for a basic vinegar and oil dressing

¼ c. parsley flakes   ¼ c. tarragon leaves
1 tblsp. oregano leaves   1 tblsp. celery flakes
1 tblsp. dill weed

With blender set at lowest speed, sprinkle parsley flakes, oregano, dill weed, tarragon and celery flakes a little at a time into blender jar. Blend 5 seconds after each addition. Place in airtight container. Makes ½ cup.

Directions to pack with herb blend: Use Salad Herbs as a seasoning for your favorite tossed salad or stewed tomatoes or use to make Tuna Triangles (recipe follows).

TUNA TRIANGLES

1 (9¼ oz.) can water-pack
   tuna, drained
2 tblsp. mayonnaise
¼ c. chopped
   pimiento-stuffed olives

¼ c. creamed cottage
   cheese
1 tsp. Salad Herbs
Toast triangles
Chopped fresh parsley

Mash and shred tuna with a fork. Combine tuna with mayonnaise, olives, cottage cheese and Salad Herbs in blender set at lowest speed for 10 to 15 seconds or until mixture is smooth.

Remove from blender and chill. Spread on toast triangles and garnish with parsley. Makes 1½ cups.

HERB SALT

This herb blend is almost as indispensable as table salt

¼ c. parsley flakes
1 tblsp. basil leaves
1 tblsp. oregano leaves

1 tblsp. paprika
1 tsp. celery flakes
1 c. salt

With blender set at lowest speed, sprinkle parsley flakes, basil, oregano, paprika and celery flakes a little at a time into blender jar. Add salt, a little at a time. Continue blending until herbs are as fine as salt. Pour into shaker. Makes 1 cup.

Directions to pack with salt: Use Herb Salt as a seasoning for your favorite meat dishes or use to make Irish Broth (recipe follows).

IRISH BROTH

2 tblsp. butter or regular
   margarine
1 lb. beef chuck, cut in ½″
   cubes
2 qts. water
½ c. pearl barley
2 carrots, pared and sliced

1 medium onion, finely
   chopped
1 c. shredded cabbage
4 beef bouillon cubes
½ tsp. salt
¼ tsp. pepper
1 tsp. Herb Salt

Melt butter in 4-qt. saucepan. Brown beef cubes on all sides. Add water, barley, carrots, onion, cabbage, beef bouillon cubes, salt, pepper and Herb Salt. Bring to a boil; reduce heat. Cover and simmer over low heat for 2 hours. Makes 9 cups.

FINES HERBS

This aromatic herb combination enhances most meat dishes

1 tblsp. ground lemon peel
1 tblsp. parsley flakes
1 tblsp. tarragon leaves

1 tsp. marjoram leaves
1 tsp. basil leaves
1 tsp. celery salt

With blender set at lowest speed, sprinkle lemon peel, parsley flakes, tarragon, marjoram, basil and celery salt, a little at a time, into blender jar. Blend 5 seconds after each addition. Place in airtight container. Makes 3 tablespoons.

Directions to pack with herb blend: Use Fines Herbs as a seasoning for your favorite soups and stews or use to make Baked Stuffed Potatoes (recipe follows).

BAKED STUFFED POTATOES

4 large baking potatoes
¼ c. light cream
1 egg, well beaten
1 c. grated sharp process
   cheese
1 tsp. salt

2 tblsp. butter or regular
   margarine
1 tsp. Fines Herbs
2 tblsp. melted butter or
   regular margarine
Paprika

Bake potatoes in 425° oven 50 minutes or until done.

Cut each potato in half lengthwise. Carefully scoop out insides with a spoon, leaving enough potato in the shells to hold their shape. Mash potatoes well, blending in light cream, egg, cheese, salt, 2 tblsp. butter and Fines Herbs. Pile mixture lightly into shells. Drizzle melted butter over top; sprinkle with paprika.

Place potatoes under broiler for a few minutes to brown and heat through. Makes 8 servings.

PINEAPPLE CHEESE BALL

Try rolling this creamy appetizer ball in shredded carrots

2 (8 oz.) pkgs. cream
   cheese, softened
1 (8¼ oz.) can crushed
   pineapple, drained
1 c. chopped walnuts

¼ c. minced green pepper
3 tblsp. minced onion
1 tsp. seasoned salt
1 c. chopped walnuts
Chopped fresh parsley

Beat cream cheese in bowl until smooth and creamy, using electric mixer at medium speed. Stir in pineapple, 1 c. walnuts, green pepper, onion and seasoned salt.

Divide mixture in half. Shape into 2 balls. Roll in 1 c. walnuts. Wrap in aluminum foil. Refrigerate 2 hours or until well chilled. Garnish with parsley. Makes 2 appetizer balls.

Directions to pack with cheese ball: Store in refrigerator. Delicious served with crackers.

BLUE CHEESE BALL

Especially good on unsalted crackers or sliced party rye

½ c. chopped walnuts	1 tblsp. chopped pimientos
1 (8 oz.) pkg. cream cheese, softened	1 tblsp. minced green pepper
4 oz. blue cheese, crumbled	¼ tsp. garlic powder

Spread walnuts in shallow baking pan.

Toast in 350° oven 9 minutes, stirring occasionally, until golden brown. Cool slightly.

Beat cream cheese in bowl until smooth and creamy, using electric mixer at medium speed. Blend in blue cheese. Stir in pimientos, green pepper and garlic powder. Chill in refrigerator until firm.

Shape mixture into a ball. Roll in toasted walnuts. Wrap in aluminum foil. Chill at least 1 hour. Makes 1 appetizer ball.

Directions to pack with cheese ball: Store in refrigerator. Serve with crackers.

CLAM APPETIZER DIP

"My guests always rave about this dip," a Maryland woman said

1 (8 oz.) pkg. cream cheese, softened	2 tsp. lemon juice
½ c. dairy sour cream	2 tsp. Worcestershire sauce
2 tblsp. minced onion	1 (7 oz.) can minced clams, drained
1 tblsp. minced fresh parsley	

Beat cream cheese in bowl until smooth and creamy, using electric mixer at medium speed. Beat in sour cream. Stir in onion, parsley, lemon juice, Worcestershire sauce and clams; mix well. Cover and chill at least 1 hour. Makes 1⅔ cups.

Directions to pack with dip: Store in refrigerator. Serve with crackers or chips.

CHEDDAR CHEESE ROLL

These attractive cheese rolls make unusual holiday hostess gifts

1 (8 oz.) pkg. cream cheese, softened
1 lb. Cheddar cheese, shredded
¾ c. finely chopped walnuts
¼ tsp. Worcestershire sauce
Paprika or minced fresh parsley

Beat cream cheese in bowl until smooth and creamy, using electric mixer at medium speed. Blend in Cheddar cheese. Stir in walnuts and Worcestershire sauce. Divide mixture in thirds. Shape each third into a 10″ roll. Roll in paprika or parsley. Wrap in aluminum foil and chill in refrigerator 3 hours.

To serve: Cut in thin slices. Serve on crackers. Makes 3 appetizer rolls.

Directions to pack with cheese rolls: Store in refrigerator. Cut in thin slices. Serve on crackers.

RHUBARB/PINEAPPLE SAUCE

This delicate pink topping has a tangy rhubarb flavor

3 c. diced fresh rhubarb
1 (8½ oz.) can crushed pineapple
½ c. sugar
½ c. water
¼ c. red cinnamon candies
2 tblsp. cornstarch
2 tblsp. water
¼ tsp. salt
2 tblsp. lemon juice
2 tblsp. butter or regular margarine

Combine rhubarb, undrained pineapple, sugar, ½ c. water and cinnamon candies in 2-qt. saucepan; mix well. Cook over medium heat until mixture comes to a boil, stirring occasionally.

Combine cornstarch and 2 tblsp. water; mix to blend. Gradually stir into hot mixture. Reduce heat to low; simmer 5 minutes. Remove from heat. Stir in salt, lemon juice and butter. Cool slightly before serving. Delicious served over ice cream or squares of cake. Or pour slightly cooked sauce into jars or bottles; cover with lids. Store in refrigerator. Makes 4 cups.

Directions to pack with sauce: Store in refrigerator. Reheat sauce before using. Serve over ice cream or cake squares.

PEANUT ICE CREAM SAUCE

Try this topping the next time you serve banana splits

1 c. dark corn syrup	½ c. milk
1 c. sugar	½ tsp. vanilla
¼ tsp. salt	½ c. chopped, roasted
2 tblsp. butter or regular	salted peanuts
margarine	

Combine corn syrup, sugar, salt, butter and milk in saucepan. Cook over medium heat, stirring constantly, until mixture comes to a boil. Boil gently 3 minutes, stirring occasionally. Remove from heat.

Stir in vanilla and peanuts. Cool completely.

Store sauce in covered container in refrigerator. Delicious over vanilla ice cream. Stir sauce before serving. Makes 2 cups.

Directions to pack with sauce: Store in refrigerator. Stir well before using. Serve over vanilla ice cream.

APRICOT SAUCE

Quite a popular ice cream topping in our Test Kitchens

2 tblsp. cornstarch	½ c. light corn syrup
Dash of ground nutmeg	2 tsp. lemon juice
Dash of salt	¼ tsp. grated lemon rind
1 (12 oz.) can apricot nectar	

Combine cornstarch, nutmeg and salt in small saucepan. Gradually blend in apricot nectar and corn syrup. Bring to a boil over medium heat and boil 1 minute, stirring constantly. Remove from heat; stir in lemon juice and rind. Store in covered jars in refrigerator. Makes 2 cups.

Directions to pack with sauce: Store in refrigerator. Serve warm on ice cream or warm gingerbread.

COFFEE/PECAN SAUCE

Pour over coffee ice cream for a double-strength coffee flavor

1 tblsp. instant coffee	½ c. dark corn syrup
2 tsp. cornstarch	1 tsp. grated orange rind
½ c. water	½ c. chopped pecans

Mix coffee and cornstarch in small saucepan; gradually stir in water. Add corn syrup and orange rind. Cook over medium heat, stirring constantly, until sauce comes to boil. Reduce heat and simmer 1 minute. Remove from heat. Stir in pecans. Cool to room temperature. Store in covered jar in refrigerator. Makes about 1 cup.

Directions to pack with sauce: Store in refrigerator. Serve cold over ice cream and/or plain cake.

TANGY CHERRY SAUCE

This fruit sauce can be made ahead and reheated at serving time

1 (1 lb.) can pitted sour red cherries	Dash of salt
2 tblsp. cornstarch	1 c. light corn syrup
⅛ tsp. ground cinnamon	12 drops red food color
	½ tsp. almond flavoring

Drain and reserve liquid from cherries, adding water if necessary, to make ⅔ c.

Combine cornstarch, cinnamon and salt in medium saucepan. Gradually blend in cherry liquid; add cherries. Stir in corn syrup. Bring to a boil over medium heat and boil 1 minute, stirring constantly. Add red food color and almond flavoring. Store in covered jars in refrigerator. Makes 2¾ cups.

Directions to pack with sauce: Store in refrigerator. Serve warm over ice cream or plain cake.

SPICY BLUEBERRY SAUCE

Makes a refreshing treat when spooned over lemon sherbet

1 (10 oz.) pkg. frozen blueberries, thawed	⅛ tsp. ground cinnamon
½ c. light corn syrup	⅛ tsp. ground allspice
1 tblsp. cornstarch	Dash of salt
1 tblsp. water	2 tblsp. lemon juice

Combine blueberries and corn syrup in medium saucepan.

Blend cornstarch and water; stir into blueberry mixture. Add cinnamon, allspice and salt. Bring to a boil over medium heat and boil 1 minute, stirring constantly. Remove from heat; stir in lemon juice. Serve warm or pour into bottles or jars; cover with lids. Store in refrigerator. Makes 1½ cups.

Directions to pack with sauce: Store in refrigerator. Serve warm over plain cake or ice cream.

EASY BUTTERSCOTCH SAUCE

This golden rich sauce is delicious served either warm or cold

1¼ c. light brown sugar,
   firmly packed
1 c. light corn syrup
¼ c. butter or regular
   margarine

¼ tsp. salt
½ c. evaporated milk
1 tsp. vanilla
½ c. toasted chopped
   walnuts

Mix together brown sugar, corn syrup, butter and salt in 1-qt. saucepan. Cook over medium heat, stirring constantly, until sugar dissolves. Do not boil. Remove from heat; cool to room temperature.

Stir in milk and vanilla, beating with spoon until well mixed. Add walnuts. Store in covered jar in refrigerator. Makes 2½ cups.

Directions to pack with sauce: Store in refrigerator. Serve warm or cold over ice cream.

THANKS FOR THE FAVOR

"I often give a friend or neighbor a jar of my homemade jelly or a loaf of freshly baked tea bread in appreciation for helping out when I really needed it." This phrase was repeated many times by farm women when they sent us their food gift recipes. Perhaps a friend helped out by baby sitting or offering to drive a child to a piano lesson or pitching in during the busy harvest season.

"I know my neighbor never expects a 'thank you' for a thoughtful gesture," an Illinois woman wrote, "but she is delighted when I drop in with a loaf of my blue-ribbon rye bread just in time for the family dinner."

Any one of the following recipes would be a delicious way to say "thanks for the favor."

FESTIVE ORANGE BREAD

This moist quick bread keeps well for several days

2½ c. sifted flour	1 egg
1 tsp. baking powder	1 tsp. vanilla
1 tsp. baking soda	1 tsp. orange extract
½ tsp. salt	1 tblsp. grated orange rind
½ c. butter or regular margarine	1 c. orange juice
1 c. sugar	1 c. chopped dates
	1 c. chopped pecans

Sift together flour, baking powder, baking soda and salt.

Cream together butter and sugar in mixing bowl until light and fluffy, using electric mixer at medium speed. Add egg, vanilla, orange extract and orange rind; beat well.

Add dry ingredients alternately with orange juice, mixing well after each addition. Stir in dates and pecans. Pour batter into greased and waxed paper-lined 9×5×3" loaf pan.

Bake in 325° oven 1 hour 10 minutes or until bread tests done. Cool in pan on rack 10 minutes. Remove from pan; cool on rack. Wrap loaf in aluminum foil and let stand 24 hours for easier slicing. Makes 1 loaf.

BANANA TEA BREAD

For a special treat, spread with softened cream cheese

2 c. sifted flour	2 eggs
3½ tsp. baking powder	2 tblsp. orange juice
¾ tsp. salt	1 tblsp. lemon juice
⅓ c. shortening	1 c. mashed bananas
¾ c. sugar	½ c. chopped walnuts

Sift together flour, baking powder and salt.

Cream together shortening and sugar in mixing bowl until light and fluffy, using electric mixer at medium speed. Add eggs, one at a time, beating well after each addition.

Blend in orange juice, lemon juice and bananas. Gradually stir dry ingredients into creamed mixture, stirring just until blended. Stir in walnuts. Pour batter into well-greased 8½ × 4½ × 2½″ loaf pan.

Bake in 325° oven 1 hour or until bread tests done. Cool in pan on rack 10 minutes. Remove from pan; cool on rack. Makes 1 loaf.

PUMPKIN DATE BREAD

Serve this spicy tea bread at your next coffee break

3⅓ c. sifted flour	2⅔ c. sugar
2 tsp. baking soda	4 eggs
½ tsp. baking powder	1 (1 lb.) can mashed
1½ tsp. salt	pumpkin (2 c.)
1½ tsp. ground cinnamon	⅔ c. water
½ tsp. ground cloves	⅔ c. chopped walnuts
½ tsp. ground nutmeg	⅔ c. chopped dates
⅔ c. shortening	

Sift together flour, baking soda, baking powder, salt, cinnamon, cloves and nutmeg.

Cream together shortening and sugar in mixing bowl until light and fluffy, using electric mixer at medium speed. Add eggs, one at a time, beating well after each addition. Add pumpkin and water; beat well.

Add dry ingredients, stirring just until moistened. Stir in walnuts and dates. Pour batter into 2 greased 9×5×3″ loaf pans.

Bake in 350° oven 1 hour or until breads test done. Cool in pans on racks 5 minutes. Remove from pans; cool on racks. Wrap loaf in aluminum foil and let stand 24 hours for easier slicing. Makes 2 loaves.

COUNTRY RYE BREAD

Serve wedges of this bread with bowls of homemade bean soup

1 c. milk, scalded
1 c. regular-strength coffee
¼ c. molasses
¼ c. brown sugar, firmly
   packed
¼ c. shortening
2 tsp. salt

1 pkg. active dry yeast
1 tsp. sugar
¼ c. lukewarm water
   (110°)
4 c. sifted all-purpose flour
2 c. rye flour

Combine milk, coffee, molasses, brown sugar, shortening and salt in mixing bowl. Cool to lukewarm.

Sprinkle yeast and sugar over lukewarm water; stir to dissolve.

Add yeast mixture and 2 c. all-purpose flour to milk mixture. Beat with electric mixer at medium speed, about 2 minutes, scraping bowl occasionally. Or beat with spoon until batter is smooth.

Stir in rye flour. Gradually add enough remaining all-purpose flour to make a soft dough that leaves the sides of the bowl. Turn out on floured surface and knead until smooth and satiny, about 8 to 10 minutes.

Place dough in lightly greased bowl; turn over to grease top. Cover and let rise in warm place until doubled, about 1 hour.

Punch down dough. Divide dough in half. Shape one half into a round loaf and place on greased baking sheet. Repeat with remaining dough. Cover and let rise until doubled, about 1 hour.

Bake in 325° oven 45 minutes or until breads test done. Remove from baking sheets; cool on racks. Makes 2 loaves.

DORIS'S RAISED DOUGHNUTS

A Vermont homemaker has surprised neighbors and friends with these excellent light doughnuts for over twenty years

2 c. milk, scalded	1 egg
⅓ c. sugar	½ c. cooking oil
1 tblsp. salt	6 c. sifted flour
1 pkg. active dry yeast	Cooking oil
⅓ c. lukewarm water (110°)	Sugar

Combine milk, sugar and salt in mixing bowl. Cool to lukewarm.

Sprinkle yeast over lukewarm water; stir to dissolve.

Add yeast mixture, egg, oil and 2 c. flour to milk mixture. Beat with electric mixer at medium speed, about 2 minutes, scraping bowl occasionally. Or beat with spoon until batter is smooth.

Gradually stir in enough remaining flour to make a soft dough that leaves the sides of the bowl. Turn out on floured surface and knead until smooth and satiny, about 5 minutes.

Place dough in lightly greased bowl; turn over to grease top. Cover and let rise in warm place until doubled, about 1 hour.

Roll dough out to ½″ thickness. Cut with floured 2½″ doughnut cutter. Place on floured waxed paper. Cover and let rise until doubled, about 30 minutes.

Pour oil into skillet or deep fat fryer, filling one third full. Heat oil to 360°. Slide doughnuts into hot oil using floured pancake turner. Fry 2 or 3 minutes or until golden brown, turning once. Drain on paper towels. Roll in sugar. Makes about 36 doughnuts.

ZUCCHINI SQUASH PICKLES

A terrific way to use up all those zucchini in your garden

4 qts. sliced unpared zucchini (¼" thick)	5 c. sugar
4 c. sliced onions	1 qt. white vinegar
2 green peppers, seeded and cut in strips	3 tsp. mustard seeds
¼ c. pickling salt	1½ tsp. ground turmeric
	1½ tsp. celery seeds

Combine zucchini, onions, green peppers and salt in large bowl. Cover with ice cubes and let stand 3 hours. (If needed, add more ice.) Drain well.

Combine sugar, vinegar, mustard seeds, turmeric and celery seeds in large kettle. Heat to boiling. Add drained zucchini mixture; mix well. Return to boiling; reduce heat. Simmer, uncovered, 3 minutes.

Immediately ladle into 8 hot pint jars, filling to within ¼" from the top. Adjust lids.

Process in boiling water bath 15 minutes. Start to count the processing time when water in canner returns to boiling.

Remove jars. Cool on wire racks 12 to 24 hours. Check jars for airtight seals. Makes 8 pints.

RHUBARB/ORANGE JELLY

Even a novice jelly maker can be successful with this recipe

4 c. diced fresh rhubarb	⅓ c. water
2 c. water	1 (1¾ oz.) pkg. powdered fruit pectin
1 (6 oz.) can frozen orange juice concentrate	4 c. sugar

Combine rhubarb and 2 c. water in 2-qt. saucepan. Bring to a boil; reduce heat and simmer 15 minutes. Drain rhubarb, reserving cooking liquid. Press rhubarb through food mill.

Add enough of reserved cooking liquid to rhubarb pulp to make 2 c. Combine 2 c. mixture, orange juice concentrate and ⅓ c. water in Dutch oven. Bring mixture to a boil. Stir in fruit pectin. Bring to a rolling boil. Add sugar all at once; boil 1 minute.

Ladle jelly into 5 hot sterilized half-pint jars. Adjust lids. Cool on wire racks 12 to 24 hours. Check jars for airtight seals. Makes 5 half-pints.

EASY APPLE JELLY

Interesting flavor combination and so easy to prepare

**4 c. bottled or canned apple
    juice
2 drops red food color**

**1 pkg. powdered fruit pectin
5 c. sugar**

Combine apple juice, food color and powdered fruit pectin in Dutch oven; mix well. Bring to a hard boil over high heat, stirring constantly. Stir in sugar all at once. Bring to a full rolling boil and boil 1 minute, stirring constantly. Remove from heat. Skim.

Immediately pour into 6 hot sterilized half-pint jars. Adjust lids. Cool on wire racks 12 to 24 hours. Check jars for airtight seals. Makes 6 half-pints.

Chapter 6

SHARE WITH A SHUT-IN

It's the little things in life that mean a lot—especially to a friend or neighbor who lives alone or in a nursing home.

"Whenever I'm feeling a little 'down,'" a Georgia homemaker wrote us, "I head for the kitchen and make a big batch of home-made soup. Then I pour it into quart jars and take it to several elderly or widowed neighbors. Suddenly the day is brighter!"

A Texas woman often took baked goods to elderly folks, but she discovered that what they really appreciated the most was a one-dish meal. So now, when she fixes a casserole for sup-per, she fills a small plastic container with enough for one serv-ing and pops it in the freezer. It's ready for taking to a shut-in along with directions for thawing and heating.

Baked goods are popular to take to nursing homes. A spicy pan of gingerbread or old-fashioned apple cakes or cookies. The recipient can share with friends. Pack paper plates, napkins and plastic forks for an extra little thoughtful gesture.

Then there is the "just thought I'd drop by with a little thought" gift. Perhaps it's a jar of homemade relish or jelly or a plate of warm-from-the-oven rolls. What really means the most to elderly people who can't get out is the fact that you took the time to remember them, a Minnesota woman emphasized when she sent in her recipe for homemade relish.

SAY HELLO WITH SOME NOURISHING SOUP

On a bone-chilling day, nothing tastes better than a big bowl of steaming homemade soup. When many farm women make soup for their families, they always think of the elderly neighbor and double the recipe.

These soups are chock-full of vitamins, minerals and protein. The Basic Beef Broth with Dumplings always makes a big hit. The plump little dumplings are filled with meat. It's a wonderful soup to tempt an invalid who doesn't have much of an appetite.

BASIC BEEF BROTH WITH DUMPLINGS

This soup features yummy Meat Dumplings stuffed with beef

5 lbs. meaty shin beef bones	10 whole peppercorns
3 tblsp. cooking oil	2 tblsp. salt
5 medium onions, quartered	½ tsp. marjoram leaves
3 medium carrots, cut in 3" chunks	1 bay leaf
	6 sprigs fresh parsley
3 stalks celery, cut in 3" chunks	Meat Dumplings (recipe follows)
3 qts. water	Sliced green onions and tops
1 clove garlic	

Brown beef on all sides in hot oil in 6-qt. Dutch oven. Remove meat as it browns. Add onions, carrots and celery; sauté 10 minutes or until lightly browned. Add meat, water, garlic, peppercorns, salt, marjoram, bay leaf and parsley. Bring to a boil; reduce heat. Skim off foam. Cover and simmer 3 hours 30 minutes.

Strain broth. Remove meat from bones. Mince enough beef to make 1½ cups; set aside for Meat Dumplings (recipe follows).

Prepare Meat Dumplings. To serve, remove excess fat from broth. Heat beef broth with Meat Dumplings. Serve soup in bowls topped with green onions. Makes 3 quarts.

MEAT DUMPLINGS

Basic Beef Broth (see
   recipe)
1 c. chopped onion
2 tblsp. shredded pared
   carrot
2 tblsp. butter or regular
   margarine
1 tblsp. cooking oil
1½ c. minced cooked beef
   (reserved in Basic Beef
   Broth recipe)

1 egg
½ tsp. salt
¼ tsp. pepper
¼ c. minced fresh parsley
1½ c. sifted flour
¼ tsp. salt
2 eggs, beaten
2 tblsp. milk
3 qts. water
2 tsp. salt

Prepare Basic Beef Broth (see recipe).

Sauté onion and carrot in melted butter and oil in small skillet until tender (do not brown). Combine sautéed vegetables, cooked beef, 1 egg, ½ tsp. salt, pepper and parsley in bowl. Mix lightly, but well. Set aside.

Combine flour and ¼ tsp. salt in bowl. Add 2 eggs and milk, stirring vigorously, until mixture leaves the sides of the bowl. (Add 1 more tblsp. flour, if necessary.) Divide dough in half. Cover ½ of dough with damp cloth.

Roll ½ of dough on floured surface to 13½" circle. Cut in 2¼" rounds. Place 1 tsp. filling on lower half of each round. Dampen edge of round with water. Fold in half, covering filling. Seal edges. Pinch two corners together making a circle. Repeat with remaining dough, making 72 stuffed dumplings.

Bring water and 2 tsp. salt to a boil in large kettle. Cook dumplings in boiling water, 18 at a time, 10 minutes or until tender. Remove from water with slotted spoon. Drain on paper towels.

Heat Meat Dumplings in Basic Beef Broth for soup. Or Meat Dumplings can be topped with sour cream and served as a first course. Makes 72 dumplings.

CHICKEN VEGETABLE SOUP

The lemon juice and beaten eggs make this soup special

1 (3 lb.) broiler-fryer, cut up	½ tsp. thyme leaves
2 qts. water	2 whole cloves
4 medium onions, quartered	¼ tsp. pepper
4 stalks celery, cut in 3" chunks	1/16 tsp. powdered saffron
3 medium carrots, cut in 3" chunks	1 c. sliced pared carrots
10 sprigs fresh parsley	1 c. sliced celery
1 tblsp. salt	2 eggs, well beaten
1 clove garlic	1 tblsp. lemon juice
1 bay leaf	Dairy sour cream
	Sliced green onions and tops

Place broiler-fryer, water, onions, 4 stalks celery, 3 medium carrots, parsley, salt, garlic, bay leaf, thyme leaves, cloves, pepper and saffron in 6-qt. Dutch oven. Bring to a boil; reduce heat. Cover and simmer 1 hour 15 minutes. Remove chicken from broth. Strain broth.

Pour strained broth back into Dutch oven. Boil, uncovered, 15 minutes to reduce stock. Add 1 c. carrots and 1 c. celery. Cover and simmer 10 minutes or until vegetables are tender. Remove chicken from bones; cut in chunks. Add to broth.

Remove from heat. Let stand 10 minutes. Gradually add 2 cups of the hot broth to eggs, stirring vigorously. Slowly add mixture to Dutch oven, stirring constantly. Add lemon juice.

A medley of gift containers. Directions in Chapter 9. Toy Train with plain and chocolate-coated Angel Food Candy (page 173) and Coconut Date Balls (page 178), Gift Canister with Peanut Butter Sandwich Cookies (page 57) and the colorful Roll Basket filled with a batch of Dot's Yeast Rolls (page 115). You will want to make them all.

Soft Pretzels (page 153) packed in a tissue-lined box would delight any dad on Father's Day. Actually these salt-studded bread twists make a delicious gift to give for any occasion. Good snacks!

Surprise your family with a Cream Puff Heart (page 142) on Valentine's Day. Make the puff the day before and, at the last minute, split and stuff with the creamy filling. Or fill with vanilla ice cream.

Christmas Gift containers. Directions in Chapter 9. Three gaily wrapped Gift Canisters, Silver Gift Box, a sassy Pink Elephant. The White Christmas Tree and Merry Santa Gift Package would make great centerpieces for a Christmas buffet table or a fireplace mantel.

Serve in bowls topped with sour cream and green onions. Makes 2 quarts.

To reheat: Place soup in Dutch oven over low heat. Do not boil.

HEARTY BEEF/VEGETABLE SOUP

You can make this homemade soup in less than an hour

1 lb. ground beef	1 c. sliced pared potatoes
1 c. chopped onion	1 c. sliced pared carrots
2 cloves garlic, minced	1 c. coarsely chopped
2 tsp. salt	cabbage
½ tsp. oregano leaves	1 c. diced unpared zucchini
½ tsp. pepper	1 (10½ oz.) can condensed
¼ tsp. rubbed sage	beef broth
1 (1 lb.) can tomatoes, cut	2 beef bouillon cubes
up	4 c. water
1 c. chopped celery	⅓ c. uncooked regular rice

Cook ground beef in 6-qt. Dutch oven. When meat begins to turn color, add onion and garlic. Cook until mixture is well browned. Drain off excess fat.

Stir in salt, oregano, pepper, sage, tomatoes, celery, potatoes, carrots, cabbage, zucchini, beef broth, bouillon cubes and water. Bring to a boil; reduce heat. Cover and simmer 20 minutes. Add rice; simmer 15 more minutes or until rice is tender. Makes about 2½ quarts.

A LITTLE HOMEMADE THOUGHT

In the country, during the busy canning season, elderly people who live alone know they will be receiving a jar or two of home-made relish or jelly. Farm friends like to share the bounty of their garden with those who are no longer able to make their own jams, jellies and relishes.

"Whenever I make homemade rolls, I rush over a batch still warm from the oven along with a pound of our homemade butter to a neighbor who can't get around and no longer bakes," a Michigan woman wrote us when she sent us her recipe for Fluffy Dinner Rolls. Another good baker packs a jar of honey in a basket along with a batch of feather-light rolls.

You might like to open a jar of your own special preserves and spoon it into our butterfly or frog decorated gift jars, featured in Chapter 9. Bake your rolls and tuck them into our gift roll basket for an extra little present.

FLUFFY DINNER ROLLS

These golden yeast rolls are also good served cold

1 c. milk, scalded	¼ c. lukewarm water
½ c. sugar	(110°)
¼ c. shortening	4½ c. sifted flour
2 tsp. salt	2 eggs
2 pkgs. active dry yeast	

Combine milk, sugar, shortening and salt in mixing bowl. Cool to lukewarm.

Sprinkle yeast over lukewarm water; stir to dissolve.

Add yeast mixture, 1 c. flour and eggs to milk mixture. Beat with electric mixer at medium speed, about 2 minutes, scraping bowl occasionally. Or beat with spoon until batter is smooth.

Gradually add enough remaining flour to make a soft dough that leaves the sides of the bowl. Turn out on floured surface. Cover and let rest 10 minutes.

Knead dough until smooth and satiny, about 10 minutes. Place in greased bowl; turn over to grease top. Cover and let rise in warm place until doubled, about 1 hour 15 minutes.

Punch down dough. Divide dough in half. Shape one half into 12 balls. Place in greased 8" round baking pan. Repeat with remaining dough. Cover and let rise until doubled, about 45 minutes.

Bake in 425° oven 15 minutes or until golden brown. Delicious served warm or cold. Makes 24 rolls.

DOT'S ROLLS

These light and tender yeast rolls will please most guests

3 c. milk	¾ c. sugar
2 pkgs. active dry yeast	1 tblsp. salt
2 tblsp. sugar	2 eggs
½ c. cooking oil	10 c. sifted flour

Scald milk in saucepan. Cool to lukewarm.

Combine milk, yeast and 2 tblsp. sugar in mixing bowl; mix well. Let stand 10 minutes.

Add oil, ¾ c. sugar, salt, eggs and 4 c. flour. Beat with electric mixer at medium speed, about 2 minutes, scraping bowl occasionally.

Gradually add enough remaining flour to make a soft dough that leaves the side of the bowl. DO NOT KNEAD. Place dough in lightly greased bowl. Cover and let rise in warm place until doubled, about 50 minutes.

Punch down dough. Divide into 4 portions. With floured hands, shape each portion into 12 balls. Arrange 12 balls in greased 8" square baking pan or 9" round baking pan. Repeat with remaining dough. Cover and let rise until doubled, about 50 minutes.

Bake in 375° oven 20 minutes or until golden brown. Remove from pans; cool on racks. Delicious served warm or cold. Makes 4 dozen.

WHOLE WHEAT ENGLISH MUFFINS

These muffins are surprisingly easy to prepare and such a special treat for those who like regular English muffins

1 c. milk, scalded	1 pkg. active dry yeast
2 tblsp. sugar	1 c. lukewarm water (110°)
3 tblsp. butter or regular	1½ c. whole wheat flour
margarine	4 c. sifted flour
1 tsp. salt	Cornmeal

Combine milk, sugar, butter and salt in mixing bowl. Cool to lukewarm.

Sprinkle yeast over lukewarm water; stir to dissolve.

Add yeast mixture, whole wheat flour and 1½ c. flour to milk mixture. Beat with electric mixer at medium speed, about 2 minutes, scraping bowl occasionally. Or beat with spoon until batter is smooth.

Stir in enough additional flour to make a stiff dough. Turn out on floured surface and knead about 2 minutes.

Place dough in lightly greased bowl, turning over to grease top. Cover and let rise in warm place until doubled, about 1 hour.

Punch down dough. Divide dough in half. Roll out one half to ½" thickness. Cut into 3" circles with floured biscuit cutter. Place rounds, about 2" apart, on ungreased baking sheets sprinkled with cornmeal. Repeat with remaining dough. Cover and let rise until doubled, about 30 minutes.

Place on lightly greased medium hot griddle or skillet, cornmeal side down. Bake until well browned, about 10 minutes on each side. Cool on racks. Makes 18 English muffins.

To serve: Split muffins in half with fork and toast. Serve with butter.

GREEN PEPPER/TOMATO RELISH

Especially good on frankfurters and mixed into baked beans

6 medium onions	6 large tomatoes, peeled and
6 large apples, pared	chopped
3 medium green peppers,	2½ c. sugar
seeded	2 c. 5% acid strength
3 medium sweet red	vinegar
peppers, seeded	1 tblsp. pickling salt

Coarsely grind onions, apples, green peppers and sweet red peppers in food grinder. Place mixture in large kettle. Add tomatoes, sugar, vinegar and salt. Bring mixture to a boil. Reduce heat and simmer, uncovered, 1½ hours or until mixture is thick. Stir occasionally to avoid scorching.

Immediately ladle into 8 hot pint jars, filling to within ¼″ from the top. Adjust lids.

Process in boiling water bath 15 minutes. Start to count the processing time when water in canner returns to boiling.

Remove jars. Cool on wire racks 12 to 24 hours. Check jars for airtight seals. Makes 8 pints.

EASY CORN AND PEPPER RELISH

This crisp colorful corn relish is perfect with most meats

1 (10 oz.) pkg. frozen whole	3 tsp. salt
kernel corn, thawed	¾ tsp. celery seeds
½ c. chopped green pepper	¾ tsp. mixed pickling
¼ c. chopped celery	spices
¼ c. chopped onion	½ c. chopped pimientos
¾ c. sugar	
1 c. 5% acid strength white	
vinegar	

Combine corn, green pepper, celery, onion, sugar, vinegar and salt in 3-qt. saucepan. Tie celery seeds and pickling spices in cheesecloth bag; add to saucepan. Bring mixture to a boil; reduce heat. Simmer, uncovered, 3 minutes. Add pimientos. Remove spice bag.

Immediately ladle into 3 hot half-pint jars, filling to within ¼" from the top. Adjust lids.

Process in boiling water bath 15 minutes. Start to count the processing time when water in canner returns to boiling.

Remove jars. Cool on wire racks 12 to 24 hours. Check for airtight seal. Makes 3 half-pints.

TANGY LEMONADE JELLY

One of the easiest jelly recipes ever and so good, too

2½ c. sugar	1 (6 oz.) can frozen
1½ c. water	lemonade, thawed
2 drops red food color	½ bottle liquid fruit pectin

Combine sugar, water and food color in Dutch oven; mix well. Bring mixture to a hard boil over high heat, stirring constantly. Remove from heat. Stir in lemonade and liquid fruit pectin.

Immediately pour into 4 hot sterilized half-pint jars. Adjust lids. Cool on wire racks 12 to 24 hours. Check jars for airtight seals. Makes 4 half-pints.

A MEAL-IN-A-DISH FOR A FRIEND

Do you know any elderly people who live alone and do very little cooking? Any one of these main dishes or casseroles would be a perfect choice to make for them.

You might like to fix a "surprise" casserole every week for a shut-in friend. That's what an Ohio woman does for an eighty-year-old friend who lives alone.

Or perhaps you could cook "double" when preparing dinner for the family some evening and make several TV dinners for elderly friends or neighbors, using the meat loaf recipe or the pork chop and bean dish given here.

When you take a main dish, include a molded salad or a bowl of assorted greens and a jar of one of our homemade dressings.

BIG RED MEAT LOAF

A moist delicious meat loaf with or without the sauce

2 lbs. ground beef
½ c. quick-cooking oats
½ c. chopped onion
½ c. chopped green pepper
2 tblsp. minced fresh parsley
2 tblsp. prepared mustard
2 tsp. salt

1 tsp. marjoram leaves
¼ tsp. pepper
2 eggs, slightly beaten
½ c. milk
Piquant Sauce (recipe
  follows)

Combine ground beef, oats, onion, green pepper, parsley, mustard, salt, marjoram, pepper, eggs and milk in large bowl. Mix lightly, but well. Press mixture into greased 9×5×3″ loaf pan. Spread with Piquant Sauce.

Bake in 350° oven 1 hour 10 minutes. Let stand 5 minutes before slicing. Makes 6 servings.

Piquant Sauce: Combine 3 tblsp. brown sugar, ¼ c. ketchup, 1 tsp. prepared mustard and ¼ tsp. ground nutmeg in bowl; mix until smooth.

PORK CHOPS AND BEANS

One woman's family asks for seconds when she serves this

6 pork chops, ½" thick	1 (1 lb.) can green lima
Salt	beans
Pepper	¼ c. ketchup
1 tblsp. cooking oil	2 tblsp. cider vinegar
¼ c. chopped onion	1 tblsp. brown sugar, firmly
1 clove garlic, minced	packed
1 (1 lb. 4 oz.) can kidney	½ tsp. dry mustard
beans	

Season pork chops with salt and pepper. Brown pork chops on both sides in hot oil in 10" skillet. Remove pork chops as they brown. Sauté onion and garlic in drippings until tender (do not brown).

Drain kidney and lima beans, reserving ⅔ c. liquid. Add kidney beans, lima beans, ketchup, vinegar, brown sugar, mustard and reserved ⅔ c. liquid. Bring mixture to a boil.

Pour hot mixture into 11×7×1½" baking dish. Top with pork chops. Cover with aluminum foil.

Bake in 350° oven 45 minutes. Remove aluminum foil. Bake 15 more minutes. Makes 6 servings.

POTATO-TOPPED MEATBALL CASSEROLE

One homemaker makes this casserole different by adding the vegetables that are abundant at the time she prepares it

1 lb. ground beef
¾ c. soft bread crumbs
¼ c. minced onion
2 tblsp. chopped fresh
  parsley
1 tsp. salt
½ tsp. marjoram leaves
⅛ tsp. pepper
1 egg, slightly beaten
2 tblsp. milk
2 tblsp. cooking oil
1 (1 lb.) can stewed
  tomatoes

1 tblsp. cornstarch
2 beef bouillon cubes
1 (9 oz.) pkg. frozen green
  beans, cooked and
  drained
1 c. sliced carrots, cooked
  and drained
3 c. seasoned mashed
  potatoes*
Grated Parmesan cheese

Combine ground beef, bread crumbs, onion, parsley, salt, marjoram, pepper, egg and milk in bowl. Mix lightly, but well. Shape mixture into 24 meatballs. Brown 12 meatballs at a time in hot oil in 10″ skillet. Remove meatballs as they brown and drain on paper towels. Pour off remaining fat in skillet.

Remove 2 tblsp. liquid from stewed tomatoes. Combine reserved 2 tblsp. liquid with cornstarch in small bowl. Mix well. Combine remaining tomatoes, cornstarch mixture and crumbled beef bouillon cubes in 10″ skillet. Cook over medium heat, stirring constantly, until mixture comes to a boil. Stir in meatballs, green beans and carrots. Heat well. Pour into 2-qt. casserole. Spread with mashed potatoes. Sprinkle with Parmesan cheese.

Bake in 350° oven 20 minutes or until potatoes are golden brown. Makes 8 servings.

*Note: Instant mashed potatoes can be used.

HAMBURGER/VEGETABLE BAKE

A rib-sticking main dish that's economical and nutritious

3 c. sliced pared potatoes
(¼" thick)
½ c. coarsely chopped
onion
1 c. sliced pared carrots
1 (1 lb.) can pork and beans
in tomato sauce
1½ lbs. ground beef
1 c. soft bread crumbs

1 (10¾ oz.) can condensed
tomato soup
2 eggs
⅓ c. minced onion
1 tsp. salt
¼ tsp. pepper
1 tblsp. horseradish
¼ c. water

Add potatoes, ½ c. onion and carrots to boiling salted water
in 3-qt. saucepan. Bring to a boil; reduce heat. Cover and simmer 5 minutes. Drain well. Arrange vegetables in greased 3-qt.
casserole. Top vegetables with layer of pork and beans.

Combine ground beef, bread crumbs, ½ of tomato soup,
eggs, ⅓ c. onion, salt, pepper and horseradish in bowl. Mix
lightly, but well. Layer meat mixture on top of pork and beans.
Combine remaining soup with water in small bowl. Spread over
meat mixture.

Bake in 375° oven 1 hour or until browned. Makes 6 to 8
servings.

HAM MUSHROOM CASSEROLE

A favorite family recipe first tasted at a church supper

6 oz. medium noodles
(3½ c.)
½ c. chopped onion
½ c. chopped celery
½ c. chopped green pepper
2 tblsp. butter or regular
margarine
1½ c. cubed cooked ham
(½")

1 (4 oz.) can sliced
mushrooms
¼ tsp. pepper
1 (10½ oz.) can condensed
cream of mushroom soup
1 c. half-and-half
½ c. milk
1 c. shredded Cheddar cheese

Cook noodles in boiling salted water in Dutch oven until almost tender. Drain. Rinse with cold water. Drain well.

Sauté onion, celery and green pepper in melted butter in 10" skillet until tender (do not brown). Remove from heat. Add noodles, ham, undrained mushrooms and pepper. Combine soup, half-and-half and milk in small bowl; blend well. Pour over noodle mixture; mix gently. Turn into greased 1½-qt. casserole. Top with cheese.

Bake in 350° oven 30 minutes or until hot and bubbly. Makes 6 servings.

CHICKEN AND STUFFING CASSEROLE

Baked chicken with yummy dressing topped with a velvety gravy

¼ c. flour	2 tsp. rubbed sage
1 tsp. salt	½ c. melted butter or
⅛ tsp. pepper	regular margarine
3 whole chicken breasts,	1 (10½ oz.) can condensed
split	cream of chicken soup
¼ c. cooking oil	3 tblsp. flour
5 c. soft bread cubes (¼")	1 tsp. parsley flakes
¼ c. minced onion	¼ tsp. browning for gravy

Combine ¼ c. flour, salt and pepper in plastic or paper bag. Add two pieces of chicken. Shake until chicken is coated. Repeat with remaining chicken. Brown chicken on all sides in hot oil in 10" skillet. Remove chicken as it browns. Reserve drippings.

Combine bread cubes, onion, sage, butter and 1 c. of the soup in bowl. Mix lightly, but well. Mound stuffing in center of greased 11×7×1½" baking dish. Arrange chicken around stuffing.

Add enough water to remaining soup to make 2 c. Stir 3 tblsp. flour into reserved drippings in skillet. Gradually add soup mixture, parsley flakes and browning for gravy. Cook over medium heat, stirring constantly, until mixture thickens. Pour over chicken and stuffing. Cover with aluminum foil.

Bake in 350° oven 1 hour 15 minutes or until chicken is tender. Makes 6 servings.

CHICKEN/NOODLE CASSEROLE

This mildly flavored hot dish will please older folks

2 (3 lb.) broiler-fryers, cut up
4 c. water
1 tsp. salt
2 c. cubed pared potatoes
1 c. sliced pared carrots
½ c. chopped celery
½ c. chopped onion

1 (10 oz.) pkg. frozen peas
1 tsp. salt
¼ tsp. pepper
⅓ c. flour
4 oz. medium noodles (3 c.)
1 tblsp. butter or regular margarine
2 tblsp. dry bread crumbs

Place broiler-fryers, water and 1 tsp. salt in Dutch oven. Bring to a boil; reduce heat. Cover and simmer 50 minutes or until chicken is tender. Strain broth and reserve. Remove chicken from bones; discard skin and bones. Cut chicken in chunks; set aside.

Cook potatoes, carrots, celery and onion in 3 c. of reserved chicken broth in large saucepan about 15 minutes or until tender. Add frozen peas, 1 tsp. salt and pepper. Cook just until peas are separated. Stir in chicken.

Blend together flour and 1 c. reserved chicken broth. If necessary, add water to broth to make 1 c. Stir flour mixture into saucepan. Cook, stirring constantly, until mixture comes to a boil.

Meanwhile, cook noodles in boiling salted water in Dutch oven until almost tender. Drain. Toss with butter until noodles are coated.

Place hot chicken mixture in greased 2½-qt. casserole. Top

with noodles; sprinkle with bread crumbs. Place under broiler, about 5″ from the source of heat, 3 minutes or until lightly browned. Makes 6 servings.

CREAMY BASIC SALAD DRESSING

Velvety smooth French-type dressing . . . good on mixed greens

½ c. salad oil	½ tsp. salt
½ c. evaporated milk	⅛ tsp. pepper
2 tblsp. cider vinegar	⅛ tsp. Worcestershire sauce
½ tsp. sugar	⅛ tsp. Tabasco sauce
½ tsp. dry mustard	

Combine salad oil, evaporated milk, vinegar, sugar, mustard, salt, pepper, Worcestershire sauce and Tabasco sauce in mixing bowl. Beat with rotary beater until smooth and creamy. Pour into jar and cover tightly. Chill thoroughly. Serve over a molded salad or tossed salad greens. Makes 1 cup.

BASIC ITALIAN DRESSING

Send a bottle of this dressing with a bag of fresh vegetables from your garden to a person living alone . . . such a surprise

1 c. salad oil	½ tsp. oregano leaves
⅓ c. cider vinegar	⅛ tsp. cayenne pepper
1 tblsp. sugar	1 clove garlic, split
1½ tsp. salt	

Combine oil, vinegar, sugar, salt, oregano, cayenne pepper and garlic in jar. Cover tightly and shake well. Chill thoroughly. Remove garlic. Shake well and serve over tossed salad greens. Makes 1⅓ cups.

A SWEET TO SERVE WITH COFFEE

"My elderly friends seem to prefer the old-fashioned cakes they remember from their childhood," an Oregon woman said. So whenever there's a windfall of apples from the family orchard, she bakes six or seven Cinnamon Apple Cakes at a time. She knows several shut-ins who will be looking forward to one of the sugar-dusted cakes and an afternoon visit.

Gingerbread, slightly scented with spices and just slightly warm, brings smiles of delight from elderly friends and it is a big favorite with the men.

Big boxes of cookies are a popular treat to take to nursing homes so that there will be lots to share with friends and nurses. An Iowa woman usually triples her recipe for Pecan Drop Cookies when she plans to visit the county nursing home. She is always a very welcome visitor!

CINNAMON APPLE CAKE

Old-fashioned apple cake that stays moist for several days

2 c. sifted flour	½ c. cooking oil
2 tsp. baking soda	2 eggs
1 tsp. salt	2 tsp. vanilla
2 tsp. ground cinnamon	1 c. chopped walnuts
4 c. diced pared apples	Confectioners sugar
2 c. sugar	

Sift together flour, baking soda, salt and cinnamon.

Combine apples and sugar in mixing bowl; mix well. Add oil, eggs, vanilla and walnuts; mix well. Stir in dry ingredients. Turn batter into greased 13×9×2″ baking pan.

Bake in 350° oven 1 hour or until cake tests done. Cool in pan on rack. Dust with confectioners sugar. Makes 16 servings.

FRESH APPLE CAKE

A New Mexico farm woman says it's the Buttermilk Glaze that makes this apple cake so extra-special

1½ c. chopped unpared apples	1 egg
1 c. sugar	½ c. melted butter or regular margarine
1¾ c. sifted flour	⅓ c. raisins
½ tsp. baking soda	⅓ c. chopped walnuts
1 tsp. ground cinnamon	Buttermilk Glaze (recipe follows)
½ tsp. ground allspice	

Place apples in mixing bowl. Sprinkle with sugar. Let stand 10 minutes.

Sift together flour, baking soda, cinnamon and allspice.

Add egg and butter to apple mixture; blend well. Stir in flour mixture; blend well. Stir in raisins and walnuts. Pour batter into greased and floured 8″ square baking pan.

Bake in 350° oven 40 minutes or until cake tests done. Cool in pan on rack. While cake is still hot, pour Buttermilk Glaze over the top. Makes 9 servings.

Buttermilk Glaze: Combine 1 c. sugar, ½ c. buttermilk, ½ tsp. baking soda and 1 tblsp. light corn syrup in 2-qt. saucepan. Cook over medium heat, stirring constantly, until mixture comes to a boil. Simmer 7 minutes, stirring occasionally. Remove from heat. Add ½ tsp. vanilla. Pour over cake.

PECAN DROP COOKIES

"I always pack these cookies in decorated coffee cans when I give them to friends in a nursing home," a Texas woman writes

½ c. butter or regular
    margarine
½ c. shortening
1 c. sifted confectioners
    sugar

2 tsp. vanilla
2½ c. sifted cake flour
1 c. coarsely chopped pecans
Confectioners sugar

Cream together butter and shortening in mixing bowl until smooth, using electric mixer at medium speed. Gradually add 1 c. confectioners sugar, beating until light and fluffy.

Add vanilla and cake flour; blend well. Stir in pecans. Drop mixture by teaspoonfuls, about 2″ apart, on greased baking sheets.

Bake in 325° oven 25 minutes or until delicately browned. Remove from baking sheets; cool on racks. Roll in confectioners sugar. Makes about 4 dozen.

SPICY GINGERBREAD

Tender-crumbed gingerbread that stays moist a few days

2½ c. sifted cake flour
1½ tsp. baking soda
½ tsp. salt
1 tsp. ground cinnamon
1 tsp. ground ginger
½ tsp. ground cloves

½ c. shortening
½ c. sugar
1 egg
1 c. molasses
1 c. hot water

Sift together cake flour, baking soda, salt, cinnamon, ginger and cloves.

Cream together shortening and sugar in mixing bowl until

light and fluffy, using electric mixer at medium speed. Beat in egg and molasses.

Add dry ingredients alternately with hot water, beating well after each addition. Pour batter into greased 9″ square baking pan.

Bake in 350° oven 50 minutes or until cake tests done. Cool in pan on rack. Delicious served warm. Makes 9 servings.

Chapter 7

ALL-OCCASION GIFTS TO PLEASE THE PALATE

A homemade specialty from your kitchen is a welcome gift on all kinds of occasions and special holidays. Maybe you never thought about how Dad might appreciate a food gift on Father's Day instead of the usual shirt and socks. Neither did some of the farm women we know until their fathers began requesting homemade favorites.

Looking for a different way to surprise the bride-to-be with a shower? Give her a recipe shower and present her with a big jar of a homemade mix for baking goodies for her new husband. You'll find a selection of versatile mixes in this chapter.

You can say "I love you" with food on Valentine's Day, just as you can wish someone a happy Easter or a joyful Mother's Day with a box of homemade candy.

And when the youngsters ring your bell on Halloween looking for a trick or treat, be prepared with some of the sure-to-please recipes in this section.

FESTIVE FOODS FOR EASTER GIVING

"My mother loves to have the whole clan for Easter dinner. Now that she is getting older, it's difficult for her to prepare the meal, so I cook an elegant dinner as my Easter present to her."

A Kansas woman sent her menu along with the above note. The main course is a Stuffed Easter Ham, coated with a delicious glaze. The dessert, Poppy Seed Torte, tastes heavenly and would make a glamorous Easter gift all by itself. Her complete Easter menu and some of the recipes are given in this chapter.

Lots of women told us that they like to give breads or candy for Easter, especially if they didn't give to all their friends at Christmas time. You'll have a hard time choosing which bread to make and give—every one is delectable. The Pineapple Cinnamon Buns, served with lots of hot coffee, would be a wonderful treat for your family on Easter morning as well as a thoughtful gift for a friend.

ELEGANT EASTER DINNER

STUFFED EASTER HAM*

GOLDEN POTATO SQUARES*

BUTTERED ASPARAGUS SPEARS

TANGY CABBAGE SLAW*

CHEESE CRESCENTS*

POPPY SEED TORTE*

* Recipes follow

STUFFED EASTER HAM

A combination of two American favorites: stuffing and ham

1 (5 lb.) canned ham
¾ c. chopped onion
¾ c. chopped celery
6 tblsp. butter or regular
    margarine
4½ c. soft bread cubes (¼")
1½ c. chopped pared apples

⅓ c. raisins
1 c. chicken broth
2 tblsp. minced fresh parsley
½ tsp. ground cinnamon
1 (10 oz.) jar pineapple
    preserves

Cut ham into 20 (⅜″) slices using electric or sharp kitchen knife. Place ham, keeping slices upright in original shape, on aluminum foil-lined jelly roll pan or shallow roasting pan.

Sauté onion and celery in melted butter in skillet until tender (do not brown). Combine sautéed vegetables, bread cubes, apples, raisins, chicken broth, parsley and cinnamon in bowl. Mix lightly, but well.

Place stuffing between ham slices, leaving 2 slices between stuffing layers. Tie stuffed ham securely with string. Cover ham loosely with aluminum foil.

Bake in 350° oven 1 hour.

Meanwhile, melt preserves in small saucepan over low heat. Remove aluminum foil. Continue baking 1 more hour. Baste with melted pineapple preserves several times during last 30 minutes. Bake until stuffing registers 165° on meat thermometer. Remove from oven. Let stand 10 minutes before serving. Makes 12 servings.

GOLDEN POTATO SQUARES

Unbaked casserole can be refrigerated ahead. Cover dish with plastic wrap because foil will cause mixture to darken

5 lbs. all-purpose potatoes	4 eggs
1½ c. chopped onion	2½ tsp. salt
⅔ c. melted butter or regular margarine	¼ tsp. pepper
	¼ c. minced fresh parsley
1 (13 oz.) can evaporated milk	1½ c. shredded Cheddar cheese

Pare potatoes and place immediately in cold water to cover.

Sauté onion in butter in skillet until tender (do not brown). Add evaporated milk; bring to a boil. Remove from heat.

Combine eggs, salt and pepper in large glass or ceramic bowl;

beat until frothy. (A metal bowl will cause potatoes to darken quickly.) Shred potatoes using medium blade of shredder. Place immediately into egg mixture, turning to coat well. Add parsley, 1 c. of the cheese and milk mixture; mix well. Turn into greased 13×9×2″ baking dish.

Bake in 350° oven 1 hour. Top with remaining ½ c. cheese. Bake 30 more minutes or until done. Cut in squares. Makes 12 servings.

TANGY CABBAGE SLAW

This crisp coleslaw has a thin delicatessen-type dressing

10 c. shredded cabbage	1 c. salad dressing or
1½ c. chopped green	mayonnaise
pepper	½ c. vinegar
1½ c. shredded pared	½ c. sugar
carrots	½ tsp. salt
¼ c. chopped onion	¼ tsp. pepper

Combine cabbage, green pepper, carrots and onion in large bowl. Toss lightly to mix. Combine salad dressing, vinegar, sugar, salt and pepper in bowl; stir to blend. Add to cabbage mixture; toss lightly. Serve immediately. Makes 12 servings.

CHEESE CRESCENTS

These rolls look so special and yet are easy to make

2 c. sifted flour	2 tblsp. grated Parmesan
3 tsp. baking powder	cheese
1 tsp. salt	1 tblsp. minced fresh parsley
½ c. shortening	Milk
¾ c. milk	
1 tblsp. melted butter or	
regular margarine	

Sift together flour, baking powder and salt into bowl. Cut in shortening with pastry blender or two knives until crumbly. Add ¾ c. milk; mix well.

Place dough on floured surface. Knead lightly 10 times. Roll into 13″ circle. Brush with melted butter. Sprinkle with Parmesan cheese and parsley. Cut into 12 wedges. Roll up each wedge from wide end. Place crescents, point down, on greased baking sheet. Brush with milk.

Bake in 425° oven 25 minutes or until golden brown. Serve warm. Makes 12 crescents.

Note: Cheese Crescents can be baked ahead. Just warm and serve.

POPPY SEED TORTE

Several generations of a Wisconsin family have enjoyed this

½ c. graham cracker crumbs
½ c. unsifted flour
¼ c. finely chopped walnuts
¼ c. melted butter or regular margarine
2 tblsp. cornstarch
2 tblsp. poppy seeds
1 c. sugar

¼ tsp. salt
5 eggs, separated
1½ c. milk
1 env. unflavored gelatin
¼ c. cold water
1 tsp. vanilla
½ tsp. cream of tartar
½ c. sugar

Combine graham cracker crumbs, flour, walnuts and butter in bowl; mix well. Pat crumb mixture into bottom and up sides, about 1″, in 8″ springform pan.

Bake in 325° oven 12 minutes or until golden brown. Cool on rack.

Combine cornstarch, poppy seeds, 1 c. sugar and salt in double boiler top. Beat egg yolks in bowl. Stir in milk. Slowly stir milk mixture into dry ingredients. Cook over simmering water until thickened, stirring constantly, about 10 minutes. Meanwhile, soften gelatin in water 5 minutes. Add to hot custard; remove from heat. Let cool to room temperature. Add vanilla.

Beat egg whites and cream of tartar in bowl until frothy. Gradually add ½ c. sugar, beating until soft peaks form. Fold custard into egg whites. Pour into cooled crust. Refrigerate until set, about 6 hours or overnight.

Can be decorated with puffs of whipped cream and jelly beans, if you wish. Makes 12 servings.

PINEAPPLE CINNAMON BUNS

"My family lines up at the kitchen door when they smell these rolls baking in the oven," says a Minnesota woman

½ c. milk, scalded	2 tblsp. melted butter
⅓ c. sugar	¼ c. sugar
¼ c. shortening	½ tsp. ground cinnamon
¾ tsp. salt	1 (8½ oz.) can crushed
1 pkg. active dry yeast	pineapple, drained
½ c. warm water	⅓ c. toasted slivered
(110–115°)	almonds
1 egg	¼ c. chopped maraschino
3¼ c. sifted flour	cherries

Combine milk, ⅓ c. sugar, shortening and salt in bowl. Cool to lukewarm.

Dissolve yeast in warm water. Add yeast, egg and 1 c. flour to milk mixture. Beat with electric mixer until smooth, about 2 minutes, scraping bowl occasionally.

Gradually add enough flour to make a soft dough. Turn onto floured surface and knead until satiny, for about 10 minutes.

Place in greased bowl; turn dough over to grease top. Cover; let rise until doubled, about 1 hour. Punch down. Let rise 45 more minutes.

Roll dough into 15×10" rectangle. Brush with butter. Sprinkle with ¼ c. sugar, cinnamon, pineapple, almonds and cherries. Roll up like jelly roll, starting at narrow side. Cut into 12 slices. Place in greased 13×9×2" cake pan. Let rise until doubled, about 30 minutes.

Bake at 350° for 25 minutes or until golden brown. Frost while warm with your favorite confectioners sugar frosting. Makes 12.

MOLASSES STICKY BUNS

Light cinnamon-swirled rolls that are perfect with coffee

¾ c. milk, scalded	¼ c. molasses
⅓ c. sugar	½ c. brown sugar, firmly packed
⅓ c. butter	
1 tsp. salt	⅓ c. butter
2 pkgs. active dry yeast	½ c. chopped pecans
⅓ c. warm water (110–115°)	1 c. brown sugar, firmly packed
1 egg	½ c. raisins
4 c. sifted flour	1 tsp. ground cinnamon

Combine milk, sugar, ⅓ c. butter and salt in bowl. Cool to lukewarm.

Dissolve yeast in warm water. Add yeast, egg and 1 c. flour to milk mixture. Beat with electric mixer until smooth, about 2 minutes, scraping bowl occasionally.

Gradually add enough flour to make a soft dough. Turn onto floured surface and knead until satiny, about 10 minutes.

A trio of handsome breads to make and give to friends at the holiday season. Clockwise from top: Christmas Morning Brioche (page 187), Christmas Eve Saffron Bread (page 183) and Regal Savarin Ring (page 188).

Give a box of Hand-painted Butter Cookies (page 179) as a Christmas gift to the friend who has everything. Gather family members around the kitchen table to paint their own original designs on the cookies. Plan to make another batch to hang on your own Christmas tree.

Gift containers. Directions in Chapter 9. Clockwise starting with Pompon Box, TV Dinner Holder, Casserole Carrier, House, Clown Favor, Frog Jar, Daisy Plate Holder, Birthday Favor, Gift Canister, Floral Gift Tag, Ghost, Pint Container, Valentine Box and Easter Basket.

A lovely gift for Mother's Day. Three homemade candies nestled in a pretty box: Homemade Marshmallows (page 147), Open House Mints (page 148) and Decorated Sugar Cubes (page 149). Easy to make, too!

Place in greased bowl; turn dough over to grease top. Cover; let rise until doubled, about 1 to 1½ hours.

Combine molasses, ½ c. brown sugar and ⅓ c. butter in saucepan. Heat until butter melts. Spread mixture in 2 greased 9″ round cake pans. Sprinkle with pecans.

Combine 1 c. brown sugar, raisins and cinnamon; set aside.

Divide dough in half. Roll each half into 12×8″ rectangle. Sprinkle with ½ of brown sugar mixture. Roll up like jelly roll, starting at long side. Cut into 12 slices. Arrange in prepared pans. Let rise until doubled, about 30 minutes.

Bake at 350° for 25 minutes or until golden brown. Invert pans on plates; remove. Cool. Makes 24.

THREE-FLAVORED BRAID

Whole wheat, rye and white bread all twisted together in one

5 c. sifted all-purpose flour	2 tblsp. molasses
2 tblsp. sugar	1 c. whole wheat flour
1 tblsp. salt	1 tsp. caraway seeds
2 pkgs. active dry yeast	1 tblsp. baking cocoa
¼ c. soft butter or regular	2 tblsp. molasses
margarine	1 c. rye flour
2¼ c. hot water (120–130°)	

Combine 2¼ c. all-purpose flour, sugar, salt and yeast in mixing bowl; mix well. Add butter and hot water. Beat with electric mixer at medium speed about 2 minutes, scraping bowl occasionally. Add 1 more c. all-purpose flour. Beat at high speed 2 minutes, scraping bowl occasionally. Divide dough into 3 parts. Add 2 tblsp. molasses and whole wheat flour to one third. If necessary, add a little all-purpose flour to make a soft dough.

Turn out on floured surface and knead until smooth and satiny, about 5 minutes. Place in greased bowl; turn over to grease top. Cover and set aside.

Add caraway seeds, cocoa, 2 tblsp. molasses and rye flour to one third. If necessary, add a little all-purpose flour to make a soft dough. Turn out on floured surface and knead until smooth and satiny, about 5 minutes. Place in greased bowl; turn over to grease top. Cover and set aside.

Add enough of remaining all-purpose flour to remaining one third to make a soft dough. Turn out on floured surface and knead until smooth and satiny, about 5 minutes. Place in greased bowl; turn over to grease top. Cover. Place all 3 bowls in warm place. Let rise until doubled, about 1 hour.

Punch down doughs. Divide each dough in half. Roll 1 portion of each dough into 15″ rope. Place 1 of each rope on greased baking sheet. Braid together; pinch ends to seal. Repeat with remaining ropes. Cover and let rise until doubled, about 1 hour.

Bake in 350° oven 35 minutes or until breads test done. Remove from baking sheets; cool on racks. Makes 2 loaves.

TRIPLE FRUIT KUCHEN

"'Please make fruit pizza again' my children often ask when I haven't made it for a while," an Indiana homemaker wrote

1½ c. warm water	Cream Cheese Mixture
2 (13¾ oz.) pkgs. hot roll	(recipe follows)
mix	½ c. drained, sliced peaches
2 eggs	Brown Sugar Crumbs
1 (1 lb. 8 oz.) jar cherry pie	(recipe follows)
filling	
1 (1 lb. 8 oz.) jar apple pie	
filling	

Pour water into a large bowl. Sprinkle in both packets of yeast from mixes; stir until dissolved. Add eggs and the flour mixture from mixes; blend well. Cover. Let rise in a warm place until doubled, 30 to 45 minutes.

Toss dough on floured surface until no longer sticky. Divide dough in half. Roll each into a 12″ circle. Place in greased pizza pans, pressing dough to sides. Make a rim around edge of pan.

Spoon cherry and apple pie fillings alternately with Cream Cheese Mixture over dough, using half for each pan. Decorate each with peach slices and Brown Sugar Crumbs.

Let rise until doubled, about 30 minutes. Bake at 350° for 25 to 30 minutes or until golden brown. Can be served warm or cold. Makes 2 kuchens, 6 to 8 servings each.

Cream Cheese Mixture: Beat 1 (8 oz.) pkg. cream cheese in bowl with electric mixer until smooth. Add 1 egg, ¼ c. sugar, ⅛ tsp. salt and 1 tsp. vanilla; beat well.

Brown Sugar Crumbs: Combine ⅓ c. brown sugar, firmly packed, ¼ c. sugar, ¼ c. unsifted flour, 2 tblsp. melted butter, ⅛ tsp. salt and ½ tsp. vanilla in bowl. Mix until crumbly.

Note: If disposable aluminum pizza pans are used, place them on baking sheets for easier handling.

EASTER KULICH

Traditional Russian Easter bread shaped to resemble the domes of old Russian Orthodox churches

½ c. milk, scalded	1 egg
¼ c. sugar	¼ c. raisins
1 tsp. salt	¼ c. chopped almonds
2 tblsp. shortening	1 tsp. grated lemon rind
1 pkg. active dry yeast	Snowy Frosting (recipe
¼ c. warm water	follows)
(110–115°)	Honeyed Butter (recipe
2¾ to 3 c. sifted flour	follows)

Combine milk, sugar, salt and shortening in bowl. Cool to lukewarm.

Sprinkle yeast on warm water; stir to dissolve.

Add 1 c. flour, egg and yeast mixture to milk mixture. Beat hard with spoon or with electric mixer at medium speed 1 minute. Stir in raisins, almonds and lemon rind. Add remaining flour, a little at a time, until you can easily handle the soft dough.

Sprinkle about 2 tblsp. flour on board and turn out dough. Knead until dough is smooth and elastic, about 5 minutes. Shape in smooth ball and place in lightly greased bowl; turn dough over to grease top. Cover and let rise in warm place until doubled, 2 to 2½ hours. Punch down dough.

Turn dough onto board and divide in half. Let rest 10 minutes. Place each half in greased 1 lb. 4 oz. can. Cover and let rise until doubled, 1 to 1¼ hours.

Bake in 350° oven 30 to 35 minutes or until well browned. Remove from cans at once and cool on rack. Frost tops of loaves with Snowy Frosting. Serve Kulich with Honeyed Butter. Makes 2 loaves.

Snowy Frosting: Mix ½ c. sifted confectioners sugar with 2 tsp. milk or cream in bowl to make a smooth frosting. Spread over tops of loaves. Decorate tops with jewel designs cut from gumdrops and candied fruit slices, or with tiny multicolored decorating candies.

Honeyed Butter: Whip ½ c. butter in bowl with electric mixer until fluffy. Gradually whip in ¼ c. honey; beat until mixture is smooth.

VERSATILE FONDANT BONBONS

To make chocolate-covered cherries, simply wrap fondant around whole red maraschino cherries and dip in chocolate

3 (1 lb.) boxes confectioners
sugar
1 c. melted butter or regular
margarine
1 (14 oz.) can sweetened
condensed milk
Assorted flavorings: almond,
maple, orange,
peppermint, lemon,
vanilla

1 (12 oz.) pkg. semi-sweet
chocolate pieces
1 (8 oz.) pkg. semi-sweet
chocolate squares, cut up
1 (2½") piece paraffin wax,
cut up
Flaked coconut
Finely chopped walnuts

Sift 2 lbs. confectioners sugar into mixing bowl. Add butter and sweetened condensed milk, mixing well. Knead in remaining 1 lb. sifted confectioners sugar. This makes 4 lbs. of fondant. Divide fondant into fourths. Flavor with desired flavoring, using ¼ tsp. for each fourth. Shape mixture into ½" balls. Candies can be dipped in chocolate, rolled in coconut or walnuts. (The amount of chocolate above will coat 2 lbs. of fondant.)

If you wish to coat fondant with chocolate, combine chocolate pieces, cut-up chocolate and paraffin wax in top of double boiler. Place over hot water; stir until melted. Place toothpick in center of fondant ball. Twirl in chocolate, coating on all sides. Shake off excess chocolate. Place on waxed paper-lined baking sheets. Let stand until chocolate sets. Candies can be stored in refrigerator or in freezer. Makes about 6 lbs.

BE MY VALENTINE

Surprise your family with a homemade valentine to eat. That's what a rancher's wife from Oregon did one year and now Cream Puff Heart is a traditional dessert every year. Members of a family in Michigan expect Strawberry Ice Cream Pie every Valentine's Day as their special treat.

Valentine's Day is a good time to remember loved ones who are away from home with something special. We have cookie recipes from Iowa, Wyoming and Illinois farm people. These are always mailed for Valentine presents. "It's a taste of home, my daughter tells me," wrote a farm woman who always mails a double batch of Butter Crispies to her daughter every Valentine's Day.

CREAM PUFF HEART

This spectacular dessert can be refrigerated overnight. Then just dust with confectioners sugar before serving

1 c. water	Cream Filling (recipe
½ c. butter or regular	follows)
margarine	2 (10 oz.) pkgs. frozen
1 c. sifted flour	strawberries, drained
4 eggs	Confectioners sugar

Fold a 9×8½" piece of paper in half lengthwise. Sketch half of a heart on it; cut out. Open paper to full heart; trace with grease pencil on baking sheet. Grease sheet lightly.

Heat water and butter in saucepan to boiling; reduce heat.

Add flour. Stir vigorously over low heat until mixture forms a ball (about 1 minute). Remove from heat.

Beat in eggs, one at a time, beating until smooth after each addition. Drop mixture by spoonfuls, with sides touching, along edge of heart outline on greased baking sheet (see photo, Plate 3).

Bake at 400° for 45 minutes. Cool on rack. Cut off top. Fill shell with Cream Filling; top with strawberries. Replace top. Dust with confectioners sugar. Refrigerate until serving time. Makes 8 servings.

Cream Filling: Combine 1 (3 oz.) pkg. vanilla pudding and pie filling mix with 1½ c. milk. Follow package directions for cooking. Cool. Then fold in 1 c. heavy cream, whipped, and 1 tsp. vanilla.

STRAWBERRY ICE CREAM PIE

Keep several of these in the freezer for drop-in guests

1 c. sugar	1 c. heavy cream
¼ tsp. cream of tartar	3 tblsp. sugar
4 egg whites	1 tsp. vanilla
2 drops red food color	2 c. sliced fresh strawberries
1 pt. vanilla ice cream	1 tblsp. sugar
1 pt. strawberry ice cream	

Sift together 1 c. sugar and cream of tartar.

Beat egg whites in bowl until stiff peaks form, using electric mixer at high speed. Slowly add sugar mixture and food color, beating until stiff, glossy peaks form. Spread over bottom and up sides of well-greased 9" pie plate, making bottom ¼" thick and sides 1" thick.

Bake in 275° oven 1 hour or until light brown and crisp to the touch. Cool completely on rack.

Soften vanilla ice cream. Spread in bottom of meringue shell. Freeze until firm.

Soften strawberry ice cream. Spread over vanilla ice cream layer. Freeze until firm.

Whip heavy cream in bowl until it begins to thicken, using electric mixer at high speed. Gradually add 3 tblsp. sugar and vanilla, beating until thickened. Spread over strawberry ice cream layer. Sweeten strawberries with 1 tblsp. sugar. Spoon strawberries over whipped cream. Freeze. When frozen, wrap in aluminum foil. Let stand at room temperature 10 minutes before serving. Makes 6 to 8 servings.

BUTTER CRISPIES

"This recipe came originally from my grandmother's Norwegian cookbook," an Iowa farm woman wrote to us

2 c. sifted flour	½ c. shortening
½ tsp. baking soda	1 c. sugar
½ tsp. cream of tartar	1 egg, slightly beaten
½ c. butter or regular	1 tsp. vanilla
margarine	Flaked coconut or sugar

Sift together flour, baking soda and cream of tartar into mixing bowl. Cut in butter and shortening until mixture is crumbly. Add sugar, egg and vanilla. Mix well.

Form mixture into 1" balls. Roll in coconut or sugar. Place on greased baking sheets. Flatten with drinking glass dipped in sugar.

Bake in 350° oven 15 minutes or until lightly browned. Remove from baking sheets; cool on racks. Makes 3 dozen.

GRANNY'S BEST OATMEAL COOKIES

Large farm house batch of raisin-studded oatmeal cookies

1½ c. butter or regular margarine	1 tsp. ground cloves
3 c. brown sugar, firmly packed	½ tsp. salt
4 eggs	2 tsp. baking soda
4¼ c. sifted flour	1 c. milk
1 tsp. ground cinnamon	4 c. quick-cooking oats
	2 c. raisins
	1½ c. chopped walnuts

Cream together butter and brown sugar in mixing bowl until light and fluffy, using electric mixer at medium speed. Add eggs, one at a time, beating well after each addition.

Sift together flour, cinnamon, cloves and salt. Stir baking soda into milk. Add dry ingredients alternately with milk mixture to creamed mixture, beating well after each addition. Stir in oats, raisins and walnuts. Drop mixture by tablespoonfuls, about 2″ apart, on greased baking sheets.

Bake in 350° oven 15 minutes or until golden brown. Remove from baking sheets; cool on racks. Makes about 9 dozen.

WHITE ALMOND FUDGE

Recycled coffee cans are perfect containers for this fudge

1 (3 oz.) pkg. cream cheese	¼ to ½ tsp. almond extract
2½ c. sifted confectioners sugar	½ c. chopped almonds
	⅛ tsp. salt

Beat cream cheese in bowl until smooth and soft, using electric mixer at medium speed. Then slowly blend in confectioners sugar, almond extract, almonds and salt.

Press mixture into buttered 9×5×3″ loaf pan. Chill until firm. Cut in 21 pieces. Makes about 1 lb.

Chocolate Walnut Fudge: Add 2 squares semi-sweet chocolate, melted, to cream cheese in White Almond Fudge. When creamed, slowly blend in 2 c. sifted confectioners sugar, ½ tsp. vanilla, ½ c. chopped walnuts and ⅛ tsp. salt. Shape 1 tsp. candy into ball and drop into small bowl containing ⅓ c. (2 oz.) chocolate jimmies. Roll ball in chocolate jimmies and place on waxed paper. Repeat until all candy is shaped into balls. Makes 30 balls.

Cherry/Date White Fudge: Substitute ¼ c. cut-up dates and ¼ c. cut-up candied cherries for almonds in White Almond Fudge. Use ¼ tsp. almond extract or ½ tsp. vanilla. Makes 21 pieces.

Coconut White Fudge: Substitute ½ c. flaked coconut for almonds in White Almond Fudge. Makes 21 pieces.

MEMORABLE GIFTS FOR MOTHER'S DAY

If you want to delight your mother on her special day, give her a box of homemade candy. Lovely to look at and luscious to eat describes the candies in this section. There are pastel Homemade Marshmallows, ultra-creamy mints and Decorated Sugar Cubes. Why not make all three recipes and arrange them prettily in a lace doily-lined box?

The rich chocolate truffles are wickedly fattening but are worth every calorie. A North Dakota woman packs these in a box covered with shiny gold paper and lined with a gold doily—an elegant gift that is easy to make.

If your mother doesn't have a sweet tooth, Golden Bread Sticks are a perfect choice. Fill a big tin with these crunchy sticks and tie with a red bow. Tuck several pink carnations in the center of the bow for an extra little thought.

HOMEMADE MARSHMALLOWS

Soft fluffy marshmallows that add so much to a box of candy

2 tblsp. unflavored gelatin	1 tblsp. vanilla
¾ c. cold water	Confectioners sugar
2 c. sugar	Chopped nuts or toasted
⅛ tsp. salt	flaked coconut
¾ c. boiling water	

Soften gelatin in cold water 5 minutes; then dissolve by stirring over hot water.

Combine sugar, salt and boiling water in 2-qt. heavy saucepan. Cook, stirring until sugar dissolves, to the soft crack stage (280°).

Pour into mixing bowl along with the gelatin mixture and beat at low speed for 3 minutes; continue beating at medium speed for 10 minutes or until mixture is fluffy and creamy. Add vanilla and pour into an 8″ square pan dusted with confectioners sugar.

Cool 30 minutes or until set. Cut in 36 squares with knife moistened in water. Roll in nuts or coconut. Place in airtight container and put in refrigerator, freezer or other cold place until ready to use. Makes about 1 pound.

Note: Tint the gelatin mixture while heating—pale green, pink or yellow—if you wish. Roll green candy in chopped nuts, pink in flaked coconut, yellow in toasted coconut and white in nuts or coconut. You can vary the flavorings if you wish. Instead of vanilla use almond, peppermint, orange or lemon extract.

OPEN HOUSE MINTS

Pack these creamy mints in silver and gold foil baking cups and place in a recycled candy box for a lovely gift

2 tblsp. butter or regular margarine	3 tsp. warm water
2 tblsp. vegetable shortening	⅛ tsp. oil of cinnamon
3 tblsp. warm water	2 drops green food color
5 c. sifted confectioners sugar	⅛ tsp. oil of peppermint
2 drops red food color	2 drops yellow food color
	⅛ tsp. oil of lemon

Combine butter, shortening, 2 tblsp. warm water and 2 c. confectioners sugar. Mix thoroughly.

Add remaining 3 c. confectioners sugar and 1 tblsp. warm water (if necessary, add 1 or more tblsp. confectioners sugar to make mixture stiff enough to roll out).

Divide mixture into thirds. To one third, add red food color mixed with 1 tsp. warm water and oil of cinnamon; knead thoroughly to mix. Roll out to ⅛" thickness on waxed paper dusted with confectioners sugar. Cut with very small cutters—hors d'oeuvre cutters with fancy shapes, if available, or use the inside of a doughnut cutter. Let the mints stand, bottom side up, on waxed paper at least 2 hours before placing in airtight containers.

To another third of candy, add green food color mixed with 1 tsp. warm water and oil of peppermint. Knead to mix; roll and cut out.

To final third of candy, add yellow food color mixed with 1 tsp. warm water and oil of lemon. Knead to mix; roll and cut out. Makes about 130 mints, or 1¾ lbs.

DECORATED SUGAR CUBES

Fill an antique glass container with these dainty sugar cubes
. . . makes the perfect gift for an antique collector

1 c. sifted confectioners sugar	Food colors
3 tsp. hot water	Sugar cubes

Mix confectioners sugar and water; add 1 to 2 drops food color to tint frosting in color desired (red for roses, blue for forget-me-nots, green for leaves—or as you prefer). Mixture should be stiff; colors should be dainty pastels.

With cake decorating tubes, make tiny flower and leaf designs on sugar cubes (see photo, Plate 8).

EASY TRUFFLES

These taste as if you spent hours in the kitchen to prepare them

2 tblsp. butter or regular margarine	1 (4 oz.) pkg. German sweet chocolate, grated
1 egg yolk	½ tsp. rum flavoring
¼ c. sifted confectioners sugar	⅓ c. chocolate jimmies

Cream butter in small bowl until softened, using electric mixer at medium speed. Blend in egg yolk. Gradually add confectioners sugar, beating well. Add German chocolate and rum flavoring, mixing just until blended. Form mixture into ½" balls. Roll in chocolate jimmies. Place on waxed paper-lined jelly roll pan. Cover with aluminum foil. Chill in refrigerator several hours to blend flavors. Makes 2 dozen.

GOLDEN BREAD STICKS

So crisp and crunchy, you'll want more than one

3½ c. sifted flour
1 tblsp. sugar
2 pkgs. active dry yeast
1 tsp. salt
¼ c. cooking oil
1¼ c. very warm water
  (120–130°)

1 egg white
1 tblsp. water
Poppy or toasted sesame
  seeds
Garlic or onion salt

Combine 1 c. flour, sugar, yeast and salt in mixing bowl. Add oil and very warm water. Beat with electric mixer at medium speed, about 2 minutes, scraping bowl occasionally. Add ½ c. flour. Beat at high speed for 2 minutes.

Gradually add enough remaining flour to make a soft dough that leaves the sides of the bowl. Turn out on floured surface and shape into a smooth ball with well-floured hands. Roll out to 10×8″ rectangle. Cut into 40 (2×1″) sticks. Roll each into 8″ rope. Arrange 1″ apart on oiled baking sheets, rolling to grease all sides. Cover and let rise in warm place 15 minutes.

Beat egg white slightly in bowl. Add 1 tblsp. water; blend well. Brush sticks with egg white mixture. Sprinkle with poppy seeds or toasted seasame seeds, garlic salt or onion salt.

Bake in 350° oven 25 minutes or until golden brown. Makes 40 bread sticks.

TO DAD ON FATHER'S DAY

A farmer who lives alone asked his daughter to stop giving him shirts for Father's Day. Instead he requested "those darn good ham loaves you make." Another father asked his daughter-in-law for a big jar of his favorite Spicy Barbecue Sauce.

Instead of buying a tie, shirt or socks, make your father a homemade food gift to celebrate his day. We have some father's favorites you might like to make and give. If he's an apple lover, you won't go wrong with the Caramel-topped Apple Pie. For a different gift, make a big batch of Soft Pretzels and wrap up a jar of mustard to slather on the top of the pretzels.

INDIVIDUAL HAM LOAVES

You'll want to try all of these unusual tasty sauces

1¼ lbs. ground cooked ham	⅓ c. evaporated milk
½ lb. ground beef	⅓ c. ketchup
¼ lb. bulk pork sausage	2 eggs, beaten
¾ c. unsalted soda cracker crumbs	Mustard/Horseradish Sauce, Mushroom/Cheese
¼ c. minced onion	Sauce or Barbecue
¼ c. minced celery	Sauce (recipes follow)
2 tblsp. minced fresh parsley	

Combine ham, ground beef, pork sausage, cracker crumbs, onion, celery, parsley, milk, ketchup and eggs in bowl. Mix lightly, but well. Shape mixture into 8 loaves. Place in 13×9×2" baking pan. Cover with aluminum foil.

Bake in 325° oven 30 minutes. Remove aluminum foil. Bake 30 more minutes. Serve with one of the following sauces. Makes 8 servings.

Mustard/Horseradish Sauce: Combine 2 tblsp. yellow mustard, 1 tblsp. horseradish and 1 c. dairy sour cream in small bowl; blend well. Serve chilled. Makes about 1 cup.

Mushroom/Cheese Sauce: Place 1 (10½ oz.) can condensed Cheddar cheese soup in 2-qt. saucepan. Gradually stir in ½ c. milk. Add 1 (4 oz.) can mushroom stems and pieces, drained. Heat over medium heat. Gradually stir in ½ c. shredded Cheddar cheese; stir until completely melted. Remove from heat. Stir in 1 tblsp. minced fresh parsley. Serve hot. Makes 2 cups.

Barbecue Sauce: Combine ¾ c. ketchup, ¼ c. minced onion, 1 tblsp. vinegar, 1 tblsp. brown sugar, firmly packed, and ½ c. water in small saucepan; mix well. Bring to a boil; reduce heat. Simmer 15 minutes. Cool slightly. Makes 1 cup.

SPICY BARBECUE SAUCE

A zesty barbecue sauce that's good on poultry or beef

1 c. finely chopped onion	2 tblsp. brown sugar, firmly
¼ c. butter or regular	packed
margarine	2 tblsp. prepared mustard
2 c. ketchup	1 tsp. Tabasco sauce
¼ c. vinegar	1 tsp. garlic salt
¼ c. lemon juice	
3 tblsp. Worcestershire	
sauce	

Sauté onion in melted butter in 2-qt. saucepan until tender (do not brown). Stir in ketchup, vinegar, lemon juice, Worcestershire sauce, brown sugar, mustard, Tabasco sauce and garlic salt; mix well. Bring mixture to a boil; reduce heat. Simmer, uncovered, 30 minutes. Cool slightly. Pour into jar; cover. Store in refrigerator. Makes 3 cups.

CARAMEL-TOPPED APPLE PIE

Makes a welcome gift and can be easily carried to gatherings

4 c. diced pared tart apples
½ c. sugar
2 tblsp. flour
Pastry for 2-crust 9″ pie
¼ c. water
¼ c. butter or regular
  margarine

½ c. sugar
¼ c. butter or regular
  margarine
¼ c. milk

Combine apples, ½ c. sugar and flour in bowl; toss until apples are coated. Arrange apple mixture in pastry-lined pie plate. Pour water over all. Dot with ¼ c. butter. Adjust top crust and flute edge; cut vents.

Bake in 400° oven 10 minues. Reduce oven temperature to 350° and bake 40 more minutes or until crust is golden and apples are tender. Cool on rack.

Combine ½ c. sugar, ¼ c. butter and milk in 2-qt. saucepan; mix well. Bring mixture to a boil, stirring constantly. Reduce heat and simmer 3 minutes. Remove from heat. Beat with wooden spoon until mixture starts to thicken. Pour over warm pie. Makes 6 to 8 servings.

SOFT PRETZELS

Taste even better when smeared with bright yellow mustard

2 pkgs. active dry yeast
1 c. lukewarm water
  (110–115°)
2 c. milk, scalded
2 tblsp. sugar
2 tsp. salt

7½ c. sifted flour
2 qts. water
1 tblsp. baking soda
1 egg, beaten
1 tblsp. water
Coarse salt

Sprinkle yeast on lukewarm water; stir to dissolve.

Pour milk over sugar and salt in mixing bowl. Cool to luke-warm. Add yeast mixture and 3 c. flour to milk mixture. Beat at medium speed of electric mixer 2 minutes. Stir in remaining flour to make a soft dough that leaves the sides of the bowl. Turn dough onto floured surface. Knead until smooth and sat-iny, about 10 minutes. Place in greased bowl; turn over to grease top. Cover and let rise until doubled, about 1½ hours.

Divide dough in half. Roll in 12×10″ rectangle. Cut into 10 (12″) strips. Roll each strip into 20″ rope. To form pretzel, hold ends of rope. Form a large loop. Twist rope once 3″ from ends. Bring down ends of rope and pinch to opposite sides of pretzel (see photo, Plate 2). Place on lightly floured surface. Repeat with remaining dough. Let rise uncovered 30 minutes.

Heat 2 qts. water in Dutch oven during last 10 minutes of ris-ing time. Add baking soda. Add pretzels to boiling water, two at a time. Boil 1 minute. Remove with slotted spoon. Let water drain off. Place pretzels on well-greased aluminum foil-covered baking sheets. Combine egg and 1 tblsp. water. Brush pretzels with egg mixture. Sprinkle with coarse salt.

Bake in 400° oven 18 minutes or until golden brown. Serve warm. Makes 20 pretzels.

Note: Pretzels can be reheated. Wrap in aluminum foil; place in 400° oven 10 minutes or until warm.

JUMBO OATMEAL/PEANUT BUTTER COOKIES

Large scrumptious cookies to please a hungry man's appetite

¾ c. butter or regular margarine	1 tsp. vanilla
½ c. peanut butter	2 c. sifted flour
1 c. sugar	1 tsp. baking soda
1 c. brown sugar, firmly packed	1 tsp. salt
2 eggs	1 tsp. ground cinnamon
¼ c. milk	1½ c. quick-cooking oats
	1 c. raisins

Cream together butter, peanut butter, sugar and brown sugar in bowl until light and fluffy, using electric mixer at medium speed. Add eggs, one at a time, beating well after each addition. Blend in milk and vanilla.

Sift together flour, baking soda, salt and cinnamon. Stir dry ingredients into creamed mixture; blend well. Stir in oats and raisins. Drop mixture by tablespoonfuls, about 2″ apart, onto greased baking sheets.

Bake in 350° oven 15 minutes or until done. Remove from baking sheets; cool on racks. Makes 3 dozen (3″) cookies.

HALLOWEEN TREATS FOR EVERY AGE

When little ghosts and witches decked out in masks and costumes ring your bell on Halloween, we think they will be happy as can be if you offer them any of the treats in this section.

And if you really want to be the hit of the neighborhood, make lots of the Halloween Ghost Party Favors featured in Chapter 9. They're easy and fun to make. Stick a ghost favor into a plastic cup filled with caramel corn to present to each child. Or invite the youngsters in to have some Pineapple Pumpkin Cake or Peach and Peanut Butter Cake—served with big mugs of cold cider.

Why not celebrate Halloween as some youngsters in a Nebraska community did? Dressed up in costumes, they visited shut-ins and elderly people and took treats—cupcakes on a bright orange plate, wrapped in foil and tied with black and orange ribbon. It was a joyful evening for people of all ages.

CARAMEL APPLES ON STICKS

Even more special when warm caramel apples are rolled in chopped walnuts or pecans

15 to 20 small red apples	**1 c. light corn syrup**
4 c. sugar	**2⅔ c. evaporated milk**

Select small apples free from blemishes; wash and dry thoroughly; do not peel. Insert recycled Popsicle sticks in stem ends.

Combine sugar, corn syrup and ⅔ c. of the evaporated milk in a 3-qt. heavy saucepan; stir to blend well. Heat slowly until sugar dissolves, stirring constantly. Then cook briskly to a thick syrup, stirring constantly.

Add remaining 2 c. evaporated milk slowly (keep mixture boiling briskly) and cook to the firm ball stage (242°). Stir constantly to prevent scorching.

Remove from heat; let stand until candy stops bubbling. Working quickly, dip apples, one at a time, in caramel syrup. Twist to remove any surplus and to make a smooth coating. Place on buttered heavy-duty aluminum foil or buttered baking sheets. (If caramel coating becomes too hard for dipping, add a little evaporated milk and reheat, stirring to keep smooth. The caramel should be kept quite hot so coating will not be too heavy.) Makes 15 to 20 caramel apples.

SURPRISE CONFECTION BALLS

A new variation of the all-time favorite popcorn balls. Wrap in bright-colored cellophane and tie with yarn scraps

28 light caramels (½ lb.)	**1 c. salted peanuts**
2 tblsp. water	**2 c. popped corn**
5 c. assorted bite-size, ready-to-serve cereals	**½ tsp. salt**

Combine caramels with water in saucepan and melt over low heat, stirring constantly.

Combine cereals, peanuts, popped corn and salt in large pan. Pour hot caramel mixture over all. Toss with two forks to distribute caramel mixture.

Press firmly into 2″ balls, dipping hands in cold water. (Be sure to distribute peanuts.) Makes about 18 balls.

CARAMEL POPCORN

Vary the recipe by adding some salted mixed nuts

6 qts. popped corn
1 c. brown sugar, firmly
  packed
½ c. molasses
¼ c. light corn syrup
¼ c. sugar

½ c. butter or regular
  margarine
2 tblsp. water
1 tblsp. vinegar
1½ tsp. baking soda

Keep popcorn warm in roasting pan in 150° oven.

Combine brown sugar, molasses, corn syrup, sugar, butter, water and vinegar in heavy 4-qt. Dutch oven. Cook over medium heat, stirring constantly, until sugar dissolves and mixture boils. Continue cooking until mixture reaches hard ball stage (260°) on candy thermometer, without stirring. Remove from heat.

Stir in baking soda. (Mixture will foam up.) Pour hot syrup over popcorn, stirring while pouring. Cool well. Makes about 1¾ lbs.

CHOCO/APPLE CUPCAKES

Delicious swirled with your favorite caramel butter cream icing

½ c. shortening
1 c. sugar
1 egg
1¾ c. sifted flour
1 tsp. baking soda
½ tsp. salt
1 tsp. ground cinnamon

½ tsp. ground allspice
1½ (1 oz.) squares
unsweetened chocolate,
grated
1¼ c. unsweetened
applesauce

Cream together shortening and sugar in bowl until light and fluffy, using electric mixer at medium speed. Add egg; beat well.

Stir together flour, baking soda, salt, cinnamon and allspice. Mix chocolate with dry ingredients. Add chocolate mixture alternately with applesauce to creamed mixture, beating well after each addition. Fill greased 2½" muffin-pan cups, two thirds full.

Bake in 375° oven 20 minutes or until done. Makes 18.

SPICY CUPCAKES

Decorate frosted cupcakes with orange candy pumpkins

1 c. sugar
½ c. butter or regular
  margarine
½ c. molasses
2 eggs
2 c. sifted flour
½ tsp. baking soda
1 tsp. ground cinnamon

½ tsp. ground cloves
1 tsp. ground allspice
¼ tsp. salt
½ c. cold coffee
½ tsp. vanilla
¼ c. seedless raisins
¼ c. chopped pecans
1 tblsp. flour

Cream together sugar and butter in bowl until light and fluffy, using electric mixer at medium speed. Add molasses and eggs; beat well.

Sift together 2 c. flour, baking soda, cinnamon, cloves, all-spice and salt. Add to creamed mixture alternately with coffee, mixing well. Add vanilla.

Coat raisins and pecans with 1 tblsp. flour; stir into batter. Pour into paper-lined 2½" muffin-pan cups, filling two thirds full.

Bake in 375° oven about 25 minutes or until done. If you like, spread tops with your favorite frosting. Makes 18.

PINEAPPLE PUMPKIN CAKE

Welcome crisp autumn days with wedges of this moist cake served with mugs of spiced apple cider

2 c. sifted flour	4 eggs
1 tsp. baking powder	1 tsp. vanilla
1 tsp. baking soda	1 c. mashed pumpkin
2 tsp. ground cinnamon	1 (8¼ oz.) can crushed
¼ tsp. salt	pineapple, drained
1½ c. cooking oil	Cream Cheese Frosting
2 c. sugar	(recipe follows)

Sift together flour, baking powder, baking soda, cinnamon and salt.

Beat together oil and sugar until well blended, using electric mixer at medium speed. Add eggs, one at a time, beating well after each addition. Beat in vanilla and pumpkin.

Gradually add dry ingredients, beating well. Stir in pineapple. Pour batter into 2 greased and waxed paper-lined 9" round cake pans.

Bake in 350° oven 35 minutes or until cakes test done. Cool in pans on racks 10 minutes. Remove from pans; cool on racks.

Spread top of one layer with Cream Cheese Frosting. Place second layer on top. Frost sides and top of cake with frosting. Makes 12 servings.

Cream Cheese Frosting: Combine ½ c. soft butter or regular margarine, 1 (8 oz.) pkg. softened cream cheese, 1 (1 lb.) box confectioners sugar and 1 tsp. vanilla in bowl. Beat with electric mixer at medium speed until smooth and creamy.

PEACH AND PEANUT BUTTER CAKE

This cake is best served the same day it is baked

1 (1 lb. 13 oz.) can sliced peaches

1 c. brown sugar, firmly packed

⅔ c. crunch-style peanut butter

½ c. butter or regular margarine

1 (18½ oz.) yellow cake mix

Sweetened whipped cream

Drain peaches, reserving ½ c. juice. Combine reserved ½ c. juice, brown sugar, peanut butter and butter in 2-qt. saucepan; blend well. Heat until mixture is smooth. Pour into bottom of 13×9×2″ baking pan. Arrange peaches on top.

Prepare cake mix according to package directions. Spread batter evenly over peaches.

Bake in 350° oven 45 minutes or until cake tests done. Cool in pan on rack 5 minutes. Invert on serving plate. Delicious served slightly warm with puffs of sweetened whipped cream. Makes 16 servings.

A KITCHEN SHOWER FOR THE BRIDE

Over the years, we have received thousands of outstanding recipes from farm homemakers. "I just received this recipe at my bridal kitchen shower," many of them wrote.

At such showers, each guest brings her favorite recipe or recipes along with a baking utensil to equip the kitchen.

A very popular present is a homemade mix. And sometimes,

the guest brings a big jar of the homemade mix, along with recipe cards for all the good things the new bride can make from
the gift mix—as well as a sampling for all the other party guests
to enjoy with coffee and punch.

We offer a choice of four great mixes with recipes for all the
variations.

There's a spicy Gingerbread Mix with directions for making
pancakes, too. All-purpose Baking Mix turns out biscuits,
muffins, doughnuts and coffee cake. You might wish to give
muffin pans, a biscuit cutter, pot holders, a recipe box or an assortment of baking pans along with your homemade mix gift.

ALL-PURPOSE BAKING MIX

*A basic quick bread mix that makes everything from light bis-
cuits to thick country-style pancakes*

10 c. sifted flour	**¼ c. baking powder**
1¾ c. sifted confectioners	**2 tblsp. salt**
sugar	**1 c. shortening**
1⅓ c. nonfat dry milk	

Combine flour, confectioners sugar, dry milk, baking powder
and salt in very large mixing bowl. Cut in shortening with pastry
blender or two knives until mixture resembles cornmeal.

Store mix in airtight containers in cool place. Makes about 12
cups.

Directions to pack with mix: Store All-purpose Baking Mix in a
cool place. Use mix to make Cheddar Cheese Biscuits, Golden
Muffins, Peach Doughnuts, Country Pancakes and Quick Coffee
Cake (recipes follow). Stir mix with large spoon before measuring. Spoon mix lightly into measuring cup and level off with
spatula.

CHEDDAR CHEESE BISCUITS

2 c. All-purpose Baking Mix
½ c. shredded Cheddar cheese
⅔ c. water

Combine All-purpose Baking Mix, cheese and water in bowl. Mix with fork until moistened. Turn dough out on floured surface and knead lightly 8 times. Roll dough out to ¾" thickness. Cut with floured 2" biscuit cutter. Place rounds, about 2" apart, on greased baking sheet.

Bake in 400° oven 12 minutes or until golden brown. Serve warm. Makes 10 biscuits.

GOLDEN MUFFINS

2 c. All-purpose Baking Mix
1 egg, beaten
¾ c. water

Combine All-purpose Baking Mix, egg and water in bowl. Stir just enough to moisten. Spoon mixture into 8 greased 2½" muffin-pan cups, filling two thirds full.

Bake in 425° oven 18 minutes or until golden brown. Serve warm. Makes 8 muffins.

PEACH DOUGHNUTS

Cooking oil
2 c. All-purpose Baking Mix
2 eggs, beaten
½ c. water
½ c. chopped canned
    peaches, well drained
Sugar

Heat oil in skillet or saucepan, filling utensil one third full.

Combine All-purpose Baking Mix, eggs and water in bowl. Stir just enough to moisten. Stir in peaches.

Drop batter by tablespoonfuls into hot oil (360°). Fry until golden brown on all sides, about 3 minutes. Remove from oil. Drain on paper towels. Roll in sugar. Makes 16 doughnuts.

COUNTRY PANCAKES

2 c. All-purpose Baking Mix   1½ c. milk
1 egg, beaten   ½ tsp. vanilla

Combine All-purpose Baking Mix, egg, milk and vanilla in bowl. Beat with spoon until smooth.

Bake pancakes on lightly greased hot griddle or in skillet, using scant ¼ c. batter for each. Makes 16 (4") pancakes.

QUICK COFFEE CAKE

2 c. All-purpose Baking Mix   ½ c. brown sugar, firmly
¾ c. sugar   packed
1 egg   1 tblsp. flour
3 tblsp. shortening   1 tblsp. butter or regular
¾ c. milk   margarine
1 tsp. vanilla   ½ tsp. ground cinnamon

Combine All-purpose Baking Mix, sugar, egg, shortening, milk and vanilla in mixing bowl. Beat with electric mixer at medium speed 4 minutes. Spread batter in greased 9" square baking pan.

Combine brown sugar, flour, butter and cinnamon in bowl. Mix with fork until crumbly. Sprinkle over batter.

Bake in 350° oven 30 minutes or until golden brown. Serve warm. Makes 9 servings.

SUPER MIX FOR BAKING

A versatile mix with exciting variations, including corn bread containing cream-style corn and wheat germ muffins with dates

9 c. sifted flour	1 tblsp. salt
½ c. nonfat dry milk	2 c. shortening
⅓ c. baking powder	

Sift together flour, dry milk, baking powder and salt into large bowl. Cut in shortening with pastry blender or two knives until mixture resembles coarse cornmeal. Store in covered container in cool place. Makes 12 cups.

Directions to pack with mix: Store Super Mix for Baking in a cool place. Use mix to make California Corn Bread, Peanut Butter Cookies, Ranch-style Biscuits, Onion/Cheese Bread, Wheat Germ Muffins, Country Supper Muffins and Spicy Breakfast Rolls (recipes follow).

CALIFORNIA CORN BREAD

1½ c. Super Mix for Baking	¾ c. milk
¾ c. cornmeal	1 egg
3 tblsp. sugar	1 (8 oz.) can cream-style
¾ tsp. chili powder	corn
½ tsp. salt	

Combine Super Mix for Baking, cornmeal, sugar, chili powder and salt in bowl; mix well.

Combine milk and egg in small bowl; beat well. Add to dry ingredients; stir just until moistened. Batter will be lumpy. Fold in corn. Turn into greased 9″ square baking pan.

Bake in 400° oven 20 to 25 minutes or until golden brown. Serve warm. Makes 9 servings.

PEANUT BUTTER COOKIES

3 c. Super Mix for Baking
1 c. sugar
1 c. peanut butter

2 eggs, beaten
1 to 2 tblsp. milk
Chocolate candy kisses

Combine Super Mix for Baking and sugar in bowl. Stir in peanut butter and eggs; blend thoroughly. If dough seems dry, add
milk. Shape mixture into 1" balls. Place, about 3" apart, on
ungreased baking sheets. Press a candy kiss in each cookie.

Bake in 375° oven 15 to 20 minutes or until done. Remove
from baking sheets; cool on racks. Makes 6 dozen.

RANCH-STYLE BISCUITS

3 c. Super Mix for Baking
⅔ c. milk

Combine Super Mix for Baking and milk in bowl. Stir about
20 strokes. Turn onto lightly floured surface. Knead lightly 10 to
12 times. Roll dough to ½" thickness. Cut with floured biscuit
cutter. Place on ungreased baking sheet.

Bake in 425° oven 12 to 15 minutes or until golden brown.
Serve warm. Makes 15.

ONION/CHEESE BREAD

2 c. Super Mix for Baking
½ c. water
1 tblsp. minced onion
¾ c. shredded Cheddar
  cheese

1 tblsp. melted butter or
  regular margarine
1 tsp. poppy seeds

Combine Super Mix for Baking, water and onion in bowl; mix
well. Stir in cheese. Pat mixture into well-greased 9" pie plate.
Brush with melted butter and sprinkle with poppy seeds.

Bake in 400° oven 18 to 20 minutes or until lightly browned. Cut in wedges and serve warm. Makes 6 servings.

WHEAT GERM MUFFINS

2 c. Super Mix for Baking	1 egg
2 tblsp. brown sugar, firmly packed	⅔ c. milk
2 tblsp. wheat germ	¼ c. chopped dates
	¼ c. chopped walnuts

Combine Super Mix for Baking, brown sugar and wheat germ in bowl; mix well.

Combine egg and milk in small bowl; beat well. Add to dry ingredients; stir just until moistened. Batter will be lumpy. Fold in dates and walnuts. Pour batter into well-greased 3″ muffin-pan cups, filling two thirds full.

Bake in 425° oven 20 minutes or until done. Serve warm. Makes 12.

COUNTRY SUPPER MUFFINS

2 c. Super Mix for Baking	1 egg
3 tblsp. sugar	⅔ c. milk

Combine Super Mix for Baking and sugar in bowl; mix well.

Combine egg and milk in small bowl; beat well. Add to dry ingredients; stir just until moistened. Batter will be lumpy. Pour batter into greased 2½″ muffin-pan cups, filling two thirds full.

Bake in 425° oven 20 minutes or until done. Serve warm. Makes 12.

SPICY BREAKFAST ROLLS

2 c. Super Mix for Baking	1 tsp. ground cinnamon
½ c. milk	2 tblsp. melted butter or regular margarine
1 c. brown sugar, firmly packed	

Combine Super Mix for Baking and milk in bowl. Mix just until dough leaves the sides of the bowl and forms a ball. Turn onto lightly floured surface. Knead lightly 10 times. Pat dough to 1″ thickness.

Combine brown sugar and cinnamon; mix well. Break off pieces of dough the size of large walnuts; shape into balls. Dip in melted butter and coat with brown sugar mixture. Place, about 1″ apart, on greased baking sheet.

Bake in 425° oven 12 to 15 minutes or until done. Serve warm. Makes 12.

HOMEMADE CAKE MIX

This mix is less expensive than purchased cake mixes and it can be used to make several different flavored cakes

9 c. sifted flour	**1 tblsp. salt**
⅓ c. baking powder	**1 tsp. cream of tartar**
¼ c. sugar	**2 c. shortening**

Sift together flour, baking powder, sugar, salt and cream of tartar 3 times. Place in large mixing bowl. Cut in shortening with pastry blender or two knives until mixture resembles cornmeal. Store in covered container at room temperature. Makes about 15 cups.

Directions to pack with mix: Store Homemade Cake Mix at room temperature. Use mix to make Chocolate Drop Cookies, Speedy Chocolate Cake, Jiffy Two-egg Cake and Grandma's Orange Cake (recipes follow).

CHOCOLATE DROP COOKIES

3 c. Homemade Cake Mix	1 egg
1 c. sugar	1 tsp. vanilla
⅓ c. baking cocoa	½ c. chopped walnuts
½ c. milk	

Combine Homemade Cake Mix, sugar and cocoa in bowl; mix well.

Combine milk, egg and vanilla; beat well. Stir into dry ingredients; mix until well blended. Stir in walnuts. Drop mixture by teaspoonfuls, about 2″ apart, onto greased baking sheets.

Bake in 350° oven 12 to 15 minutes or until done. Remove from baking sheets; cool on racks. Makes 4 dozen.

SPEEDY CHOCOLATE CAKE

3 c. Homemade Cake Mix	2 eggs
1½ c. sugar	1 tsp. vanilla
½ c. baking cocoa	Fast-fix Chocolate Frosting
1¼ c. milk	(recipe follows)

Combine Homemade Cake Mix, sugar and cocoa in mixing bowl. Add 1 c. of the milk. Beat with electric mixer at medium speed 1 minute, scraping bowl occasionally. Add remaining ¼ c. milk, eggs and vanilla. Beat 2 more minutes, scraping bowl occasionally. Spread batter in 2 greased and waxed paper-lined 8″ round cake pans.

Bake in 375° oven 25 minutes or until cakes test done. Cool in pans on racks 10 minutes. Remove from pans; cool on racks. Spread with Fast-fix Chocolate Frosting between layers. Then frost sides and top of cake. Makes 10 servings.

Fast-fix Chocolate Frosting: Combine ⅓ c. soft butter or regular margarine, 3 (1 oz.) squares unsweetened chocolate, melted and cooled, 3 c. sifted confectioners sugar, 1 tsp. vanilla and 3 tblsp. milk in bowl. Beat with electric mixer at medium speed until smooth and of spreading consistency. Add more milk if needed.

JIFFY TWO-EGG CAKE

3 c. Homemade Cake Mix	2 eggs
1¼ c. sugar	1 tsp. vanilla
1 c. milk	

Combine Homemade Cake Mix and sugar in mixing bowl.
Add ¾ c. of the milk. Beat with electric mixer at medium speed 1 minute, scraping bowl occasionally. Add remaining ¼ c. milk, eggs and vanilla. Beat 2 more minutes, scraping bowl occasionally. Spread batter in 2 greased and waxed paper-lined 8″ round cake pans.
Bake in 375° oven 25 minutes or until cakes test done. Cool in pans on racks 10 minutes. Remove from pans; cool on racks. Frost cake layers with your favorite frosting. Makes 2 (8″) layers.

GRANDMA'S ORANGE CAKE

3 c. Homemade Cake Mix	2 eggs
1½ c. sugar	Easy Orange Frosting
2 tsp. grated orange rind	(recipe follows)
Juice of 1 orange	

Combine Homemade Cake Mix, sugar and orange rind in mixing bowl. Add enough water to orange juice to make 1 c. Add ¾ c. of orange liquid. Beat with electric mixer at medium speed 1 minute, scraping bowl occasionally. Add remaining ¼ c. orange liquid and eggs. Beat 2 more minutes, scraping bowl occasionally. Spread batter in 2 greased and waxed paper-lined 8″ round cake pans.

Bake in 375° oven 25 minutes or until cakes test done. Cool in pans on racks 10 minutes. Remove from pans; cool on racks. Spread Easy Orange Frosting between layers. Then frost sides and top of cake. Makes 10 servings.

Easy Orange Frosting: Combine ⅓ c. soft butter or regular margarine, 3 c. sifted confectioners sugar, 2 tsp. grated orange rind and 3 tblsp. orange juice in bowl. Beat with electric mixer at medium speed until smooth and of spreading consistency. Add more juice if needed.

GINGERBREAD MIX

Gingerbread fans are sure to like the cake and pancakes. Why not pack mix in a baking pan with a pancake turner attached

8 c. sifted flour	1 tblsp. salt
2¼ c. sugar	2½ tsp. baking soda
3 tblsp. ground ginger	1 tsp. ground cloves
3 tblsp. ground cinnamon	2¼ c. shortening
2 tblsp. baking powder	

Sift together flour, sugar, ginger, cinnamon, baking powder, salt, baking soda and cloves 2 times. Place in large mixing bowl. Cut in shortening with pastry blender or two knives until mixture resembles cornmeal. Store in covered container in refrigerator. Mix will keep up to 3 months. Makes about 12 cups.

Directions to pack with mix: Store Gingerbread Mix in refrigerator up to 3 months. Use mix to make Gingerbread Pancakes and Country Gingerbread (recipes follow).

GINGERBREAD PANCAKES

2 c. Gingerbread Mix   ⅓ c. molasses
1 egg, beaten   ⅔ c. milk

Combine Gingerbread Mix, egg, molasses and milk in bowl. Stir just enough to moisten. Batter will be lumpy. Bake on heated greased griddle. Makes 2 dozen.

COUNTRY GINGERBREAD

2 c. Gingerbread Mix   ½ c. molasses
1 egg, beaten   ½ c. boiling water

Combine Gingerbread Mix, egg, molasses and boiling water in bowl. Blend until smooth. Pour into greased 8″ square baking pan.

Bake in 350° oven 35 minutes or until cake tests done. Serve warm. Makes 6 servings.

Chapter 8

CHRISTMAS GIFTS . . . EVERY ONE A HOLIDAY JEWEL

For good farm cooks all over the country, baking holiday foods to give as gifts is as traditional as trimming the giant Christmas tree.

We have a medley of some of the very best holiday recipes from farm women to help make your Christmas gifting the merriest ever.

There are gorgeous breads, drizzled with icing and decorated with bright cherries and nuts, and cookies of all types, including a recipe for delicate lemon-flavored butter cookies that you make and then hand paint with Christmas scenes.

After you have made all of the recipes for giving, turn to Chapter 9 and make some of our original containers for your gifts. In fact, if you're preparing for a Christmas bazaar in your community, you might want to make several of these containers to sell at your booth—we bet they will be sold out in the first hour.

MERRY CHRISTMAS CANDIES AND COOKIES

Candies and cookies are made in volume by farm women to give as homemade thoughts to the mailman, Sunday school teacher and grain elevator operator as well as to family and friends.

You'll enjoy making the selection of candies. They vary from the no-bake morsels that are a snap to make to the old-fashioned Angel Food Candy that literally melts on your tongue.

An Iowa farm woman tells us she makes at least twenty-five Holiday Wreaths to give as Christmas gifts. They make pretty centerpieces and are delicious to eat. And best of all, they are very easy to make. Her youngsters help to put them together. Even her two-year-old can assist by pushing candied cherries into the wreath.

Perhaps you would like to start a family project this year by making and decorating the Hand-painted Butter Cookies. Plan on making lots, some to hang on your Christmas tree and some to give folks on your most special Christmas list.

ANGEL FOOD CANDY

This popular "sponge" candy is so easy to make and delicious

2 c. light corn syrup
2 c. brown sugar, firmly
  packed
4 tsp. baking soda
4 (1 oz.) squares semi-sweet
  chocolate, cut up

1 (12 oz.) pkg. semi-sweet
  chocolate pieces
¼ c. butter or regular
  margarine
1 (2½×3″) piece paraffin
  wax, cut up

Combine corn syrup and brown sugar in 4-qt. heavy Dutch oven. Cook over medium heat, stirring constantly, until mixture boils. Continue cooking until mixture reaches hard crack stage (300°) on candy thermometer, stirring occasionally. Remove from heat. Carefully stir in baking soda. (Mixture will foam up.) Pour mixture at once into greased 13×9×2″ baking pan. When cool, turn out of pan. Break into pieces using meat mallet or wooden spoon.

Combine semi-sweet chocolate, chocolate pieces, butter and paraffin wax in top of double boiler. Place over simmering water, stirring until melted. Remove from heat, but keep over hot water. Dip candy into chocolate using large cooking fork. Place on waxed paper-lined baking sheets. Let stand until chocolate is set.

Store candy in cool place in covered containers. If you wish, do not coat candy with chocolate. Candy can be stored several months in freezer. Makes 3 lbs.

HOLIDAY WREATH

Place a candle in the center for a festive centerpiece

30 marshmallows	1 tsp. vanilla
½ c. butter or regular margarine	2 tsp. green food color
	3½ c. corn flakes

Combine marshmallows, butter, vanilla and food color (2 tsp. is correct) in top of double boiler. Heat over water until marshmallows and butter are melted, stirring frequently.

Gradually stir in corn flakes. Shape mixture into 9" wreath, using hands.

If you wish, decorate with red candied cherries and silver dragées. Makes 1 (9") wreath.

CANDY STRAWBERRIES

Looks so attractive arranged in a tissue-lined small basket

2 (3 oz.) pkgs. strawberry flavor gelatin	½ tsp. vanilla
1 c. ground pecans	Red decorating sugar
1 c. flaked coconut	Sliced blanched almonds
¾ c. sweetened condensed milk	Green food color

Combine strawberry gelatin, pecans and coconut in bowl. Stir in sweetened condensed milk and vanilla; mix well. Cover and chill 1 hour. Shape into strawberries. Roll in red sugar. Tint sliced almonds with green food color and insert in tops of "berries" to form leaves. Makes about 1 lb.

NAPOLEON CREMES

Rich little morsels with a deep delicious chocolate flavor

½ c. butter or regular
   margarine
¼ c. sugar
¼ c. baking cocoa
1 tsp. vanilla
1 egg, slightly beaten
2 c. graham cracker crumbs
1 c. flaked coconut
½ c. butter or regular
   margarine

3 tblsp. milk
1 (3¾ oz.) pkg. vanilla
   instant pudding mix
2 c. sifted confectioners
   sugar
1 (6 oz.) pkg. semi-sweet
   chocolate pieces
2 tblsp. butter or regular
   margarine

Combine ½ c. butter, sugar, cocoa and vanilla in top of double boiler. Cook over simmering water until butter melts. Stir in egg. Continue cooking, stirring constantly, 3 minutes or until mixture is thick. Blend in graham cracker crumbs and coconut. Press into buttered 9″ square pan.

Cream ½ c. butter in bowl using electric mixer at medium speed. Add milk, pudding mix and confectioners sugar. Beat until fluffy. Spread evenly over crust. Cover and chill in refrigerator until firm.

Melt chocolate pieces and 2 tblsp. butter in double boiler top over simmering water. Cool slightly and spread over pudding layer. Chill in refrigerator. Cut in 2×¾″ bars. Makes about 44 candies.

CHOCOLATE-COVERED PEANUTS

Chopped walnuts or pecans are also good fixed this way

1 (6 oz.) pkg. semi-sweet
   chocolate pieces
¼ c. light corn syrup

1 tblsp. water
2 c. salted peanuts

Combine chocolate pieces, corn syrup and water in double boiler top. Place over hot water; stir until melted. Remove from heat. Add peanuts; stir until coated.

Drop mixture by teaspoonfuls onto waxed paper-lined baking sheets. Cover with aluminum foil. Chill in refrigerator until firm. Makes about 36.

CHOCOLATE CHRISTMAS CANDIES

Two of our staff members can't wait to taste foods containing peanut butter. So these candies didn't last long

1 c. butter or regular
   margarine
½ c. cream-style peanut
   butter
2⅓ c. graham cracker
   crumbs
2 c. sifted confectioners
   sugar

2 c. flaked coconut
1 c. chopped walnuts
1 (6 oz.) pkg. semi-sweet
   chocolate pieces
1 (2½″) piece paraffin wax,
   cut up

Combine butter and peanut butter in 2-qt. saucepan. Cook over medium heat, stirring constantly, until melted. Remove from heat.

Combine graham cracker crumbs, confectioners sugar, coconut and walnuts in bowl. Pour peanut butter mixture over all; toss until blended. Shape mixture into ½″ balls. Place on waxed paper-lined baking sheets. Cover with aluminum foil. Chill in refrigerator.

Combine chocolate pieces and paraffin wax in top of double boiler. Place over hot water; stir until melted. Dip balls in chocolate. Place on waxed paper-lined baking sheets. Let stand until chocolate is set. Cover with aluminum foil and store in refrigerator. Makes 2 lbs. or about 8 dozen candies.

PEANUT BUTTER CANDY SQUARES

A favorite homemade American candy for years . . . now made with peanut butter. A great treat that is so easy to make

4 c. toasted rice cereal	1 (7 oz.) jar marshmallow
¼ c. butter or regular	creme
margarine	⅓ c. peanut butter

Heat rice cereal on 15½×10½×1" jelly roll pan in 350° oven 10 minutes.

Meanwhile, combine butter, marshmallow creme and peanut butter in top of double boiler. Place over hot water; stir until mixture is melted. Remove from heat.

Place cereal in buttered large bowl. Pour peanut butter mixture over all. Mix well. Turn mixture into aluminum foil-lined 9" square baking pan. Press in even layer. Cool and cut in 36 (1½") squares. Makes 36.

BEST-EVER CHOCOLATE FUDGE

This large batch of fudge will make a lot of holiday gifts

1 c. butter or regular	8 (1½ oz.) milk chocolate
margarine	bars, broken in pieces
4½ c. sugar	1 (12 oz.) pkg. semi-sweet
1 (7 oz.) jar marshmallow	chocolate pieces
creme	2 c. chopped walnuts
1 (14½ oz.) can evaporated	
milk	

Combine butter, sugar, marshmallow creme and evaporated milk in 3-qt. heavy saucepan. Cook over medium heat, stirring constantly, until sugar dissolves and mixture comes to a boil. Boil steadily over low heat 7 minutes, stirring occasionally. (The saucepan will almost be full of cooking mixture.) Remove from heat. Add milk chocolate bars, chocolate pieces and walnuts; stir until chocolate is melted and mixture is blended.

Pour at once into 2 lightly buttered 9″ square baking pans. While warm, mark candy in each pan in 64 pieces. When cool and firm, cut in squares. Makes about 5½ lbs.

COCONUT DATE BALLS

This crunchy candy requires no candy thermometer . . . so easy

1 c. chopped dates	1 c. corn flakes
½ c. sugar	1 c. toasted rice cereal
¼ c. soft butter or regular margarine	1 tsp. vanilla
2 eggs, well beaten	3 tblsp. orange-flavored breakfast drink powder
1 c. coarsely chopped walnuts	

Combine dates, sugar, butter and eggs in heavy 10″ skillet; mix with spoon. Cook over medium heat, stirring constantly, until thickened (about 10 minutes). Remove from heat. Stir in walnuts, corn flakes, rice cereal, vanilla and drink powder; mix well. Cool slightly.

With buttered hands, shape into 1″ balls. Roll in coconut. Store in covered containers. Confections can be frozen. Makes 40.

Directions to pack with candy: Store in covered container up to 2 weeks or freeze for longer storage.

GRAHAM CRACKER ROLLS

No-cook candy filled with lots of walnuts, dates and cherries

4 c. graham cracker crumbs	1½ c. heavy cream,
4 c. miniature	whipped
marshmallows	1 (6 oz.) pkg. semi-sweet
2 c. chopped walnuts	chocolate pieces
1 lb. pitted dates, cut up	2 tblsp. shortening
1 c. whole red candied	
cherries	

Combine graham cracker crumbs, marshmallows, walnuts, dates and candied cherries in bowl. Fold in whipped cream; knead to mix well. Shape into 2 rolls, about 2" in diameter and 14" long. Wrap in aluminum foil. Chill in refrigerator 24 hours.

Melt chocolate pieces and shortening in double boiler top over hot water. Coat rolls with chocolate; place on waxed paper-lined baking sheet. Let chocolate set. Cover with aluminum foil. Store in refrigerator. To serve: Cut in slices. Makes 3¾ lbs.

HAND-PAINTED BUTTER COOKIES

A fun holiday project the whole family can do together

1½ c. butter or regular	1 tsp. grated lemon rind
margarine	4½ c. sifted flour
1 c. sugar	¼ tsp. salt
2 eggs	

Cream together butter and sugar in bowl until light and fluffy, using electric mixer at medium speed. Add eggs and lemon rind; beat well.

Sift together flour and salt. Gradually add to creamed mixture, mixing well. Cover and chill dough 3 to 4 hours.

Roll out dough on lightly floured surface to ⅛″ thickness. Cut in desired shapes with floured cookie cutters. Place, about 2″ apart, on greased baking sheets.

Bake in 400° oven 6 to 8 minutes or until golden brown. Remove baking sheets from oven. If cookies will be used as tree decorations, twist a small hole in the top of each cookie with a toothpick. Cool slightly. Remove cookies from baking sheets; cool on racks. Makes 6 dozen.

To decorate cookies: Pour food color in small saucers. Add a few drops of water. You can make many beautiful colors by mixing the basic colors. Use narrow brushes for fine lines and wider brushes for large areas. Rinse brush out in water when you change colors so that your colors will be clear and not murky. With colors of your choice, paint your own original designs on the cookies.

To hang cookies on the tree, draw narrow colored cord through the hole in each cookie.

DANISH SUGAR COOKIES

This treasured heirloom recipe has been served for years during the Christmas holidays

1 c. butter or regular margarine	2 c. sifted flour
¼ c. sugar	¼ tsp. salt
2 tsp. vanilla	1 c. chopped walnuts
	Confectioners sugar

Cream together butter and sugar in mixing bowl until light and fluffy, using electric mixer at medium speed. Beat in vanilla.

Sift together flour and salt. Gradually add to creamed mixture, mixing well. Stir in walnuts. Shape dough in 1″ balls. Place about 2″ apart on greased baking sheets.

Bake in 350° oven 12 minutes or until golden brown. Remove from baking sheets; cool on racks. Roll cookies in confectioners sugar. Makes about 3½ dozen.

ICED AMBROSIA DROPS

Old-fashioned fruitcake cookies with a hint of spice

½ c. butter or regular
    margarine
½ c. brown sugar, firmly
    packed
2 eggs
1¼ c. sifted flour
½ tsp. baking powder
½ tsp. salt

½ tsp. ground cinnamon
½ tsp. ground cloves
½ c. raisins
½ c. mixed candied fruit
½ c. chopped dates
½ c. chopped walnuts
Vanilla Icing (recipe
    follows)

Cream together butter and brown sugar in mixing bowl until light and fluffy, using electric mixer at medium speed. Add eggs, one at a time, beating well after each addition.

Sift together flour, baking powder, salt, cinnamon and cloves. Gradually stir into creamed mixture. Stir in raisins, candied fruit, dates and walnuts. Drop mixture by teaspoonfuls, about 2″ apart, on greased baking sheets.

Bake in 375° oven 8 to 10 minutes or until golden brown. Remove from baking sheets; cool on racks. Frost with Vanilla Icing. Makes about 3 dozen.

Vanilla Icing: Combine 1 c. confectioners sugar, 1 tblsp. milk and ½ tsp. vanilla in bowl; beat until smooth.

HOLIDAY FRUIT BARS

Rich fruit-filled bars with a candylike brown sugar crust

1⅓ c. sifted flour
¾ tsp. baking powder
¼ tsp. salt
½ c. brown sugar, firmly
  packed
½ c. butter or regular
  margarine
2 tblsp. water
3 eggs
¼ c. brown sugar, firmly
  packed

¼ c. melted butter or
  regular margarine
½ c. raisins
½ c. golden raisins
2 tblsp. chopped red
  candied cherries
2 tsp. grated lemon rind
⅛ tsp. ground allspice
⅛ tsp. ground cinnamon

Sift together flour, baking powder and salt into bowl. Mix in ½ c. brown sugar. Cut in ½ c. butter with pastry blender or two knives until mixture is crumbly. Stir in water. Press mixture into bottom of 13×9×2″ baking pan.

Bake in 350° oven 15 minutes or until golden brown.

Meanwhile, beat eggs in bowl until well blended, using electric mixer at medium speed. Beat in ¼ c. brown sugar and ¼ c. melted butter; blend well. Stir in both raisins, candied cherries, lemon rind, allspice and cinnamon. Spread mixture over baked crust.

Bake in 350° oven 15 more minutes. Cool in pan on rack. Cut into 24 (2×1½″) bars. Makes 24 bars.

FESTIVE BREADS, DESSERTS AND CONSERVES

The week after Thanksgiving most farm women riffle through their Christmas recipe files and start on their Christmas bread baking. By early December, freezers are full of breads for holiday gift-giving.

You will want to add some of these extraordinary breads to your Christmas baking list.

For those who like to give a tangy cranberry relish as a gift, try Holiday Cranberry Relish from Pennsylvania. This is delicious and simple to make, the recipe contributor told us. She makes up at least twenty batches early in November to give as her cheery Christmas thought.

The two glamorous Christmas desserts, Festive Holiday Dessert and Ambrosia Dessert Bowl, are splendid to serve to drop-in guests or to give as a very different gift along with a handsome antique bowl in which the dessert is made.

CHRISTMAS EVE SAFFRON BREAD

Saffron gives this holiday bread a lovely yellow color and a subtle different flavor

1 c. milk	1 egg
½ c. sugar	½ tsp. ground cardamom
2 tblsp. butter or regular margarine	4¼ c. sifted flour
½ tsp. salt	Icing (recipe follows)
1/16 tsp. powdered saffron	Candied red and green cherries
1 pkg. active dry yeast	Toasted slivered almonds
¼ c. lukewarm water (110–115°)	

Scald milk in saucepan. Pour over sugar, butter, salt and saffron in mixing bowl. Cool to lukewarm.

Sprinkle yeast on lukewarm water; stir to dissolve. Add yeast, egg, cardamom and 1 c. flour to milk mixture. Beat with electric mixer at medium speed until smooth, about 2 minutes, scraping bowl occasionally.

Gradually stir in enough remaining flour to make a soft dough that leaves the sides of the bowl. Turn out on floured surface and knead until smooth and satiny, about 5 minutes.

Place dough in lightly greased bowl; turn over to grease top. Cover and let rise in warm place until doubled, about 1½ hours.

Divide dough in thirds. Shape each portion into 21″ strip. Place 3 strips on a greased baking sheet. Braid strips together; pinch ends to seal. Cover and let rise until doubled, about 1 hour.

Bake in 350° oven 25 minutes or until golden brown. Remove from baking sheet; cool on rack. Drizzle with Icing. Decorate with cherries and almonds. Makes 1 loaf.

Icing: Combine 1 c. sifted confectioners sugar, 1 tblsp. milk and ½ tsp. vanilla in bowl. Beat until smooth.

CINNAMON WALNUT TWIST

This festive bread looks braided, but is actually easier to do

¾ c. milk, scalded
1 c. butter or regular margarine
⅓ c. sugar
½ tsp. salt
1 pkg. active dry yeast
2 tblsp. sugar
¼ c. lukewarm water (110–115°)
4½ c. sifted flour
2 eggs
½ tsp. grated lemon rind

½ c. mixed candied fruit
½ c. raisins
1 c. brown sugar, firmly packed
1 c. chopped walnuts
1 tsp. ground cinnamon
⅓ c. melted butter or regular margarine
Vanilla Glaze (recipe follows)
Red candied cherries
Pecan halves

Combine milk, 1 c. butter, ⅓ c. sugar and salt in mixing bowl. Cool to lukewarm.

Sprinkle yeast and 2 tblsp. sugar on lukewarm water; stir to dissolve. Add yeast and 1 c. flour to milk mixture. Beat with electric mixer at medium speed 2 minutes, scraping bowl occasionally. Or beat with spoon until batter is smooth. Add eggs and lemon rind; beat well. Stir in candied fruit and raisins. Gradually add enough flour to make a soft dough that leaves the sides of the bowl. Turn onto floured surface; knead until smooth, about 8 minutes. Place dough in greased bowl. Cover and let rise in warm place until doubled, about 2 hours.

Combine brown sugar, walnuts and cinnamon; mix well.

Divide dough in half. Roll each half into 12×10″ rectangle. Brush with half of ⅓ c. melted butter. Sprinkle with half of cinnamon-walnut mixture. Fold dough in thirds lengthwise by folding from one side to center and then fold opposite side over, making 3 layers. Place on greased baking sheet. Cut a lengthwise slit through center of folded dough to within 2″ of each end. To give bread a twisted look, fold one end up and pull end down through slit. Then fold other end down and pull up through slit. Repeat with remaining dough. Cover and let rise until doubled, about 45 minutes.

Bake in 375° oven 30 minutes or until done. Remove from baking sheets; cool on racks. While warm, spread with Vanilla Glaze. Decorate coffee cakes with red candied cherries and pecan halves. Makes 2 stollens.

Vanilla Glaze: Combine 1½ c. sifted confectioners sugar, 3 tblsp. milk and 1 tsp. vanilla in bowl; mix until smooth.

CHRISTMAS STAR COFFEE CAKE

These attractive Christmas breads are well worth the extra time, and your guests will surely ask for the recipe

1 c. milk, scalded	3 c. chopped pecans
⅓ c. butter or regular margarine	1½ c. chopped red candied cherries
½ c. sugar	1 c. honey
1 tsp. salt	Melted butter or regular margarine
½ tsp. ground cardamom	Vanilla Frosting (recipe follows)
2 pkgs. active dry yeast	Red and green candied cherries
¼ c. lukewarm water (110–115°)	Pecan halves
4½ c. sifted flour	
1 egg	

Combine milk, ⅓ c. butter, sugar, salt and cardamom in mixing bowl. Cool to lukewarm.

Sprinkle yeast on lukewarm water; stir to dissolve. Add yeast and 1 c. flour to milk mixture. Beat with electric mixer at medium speed 2 minutes, scraping bowl occasionally. Or beat with spoon until batter is smooth. Add egg; beat well. Gradually add enough flour to make a soft dough that leaves the sides of the bowl. Turn onto floured surface; knead until smooth, about 8 minutes. Place dough in greased bowl. Cover and let rise in a warm place until doubled, about 1½ hours.

Punch down dough. Let rest 10 minutes.

Combine pecans, candied cherries and honey in bowl; mix well. (Use half of cherry filling in each coffee cake.) Divide dough in half. Roll one half into 14" circle. Place on greased baking sheet. To form 6-pointed star coffee cake, cut 6 (3") slits in circle as you would cut a pie into wedges. (Do not cut through to the center, only cut slits 3" long.) Brush dough with melted butter. Spread 1 heaping tablespoon of cherry filling, about ½" from edge of circle, in each of the 6 "wedges." To shape star point, fold one corner of wedge over filling. Then fold other corner over. Repeat folding procedure for all 6 points of star. Spread remaining half of cherry filling in center of star. Repeat with remaining dough. Cover and let rise until doubled, about 30 minutes.

Bake in 350° oven 25 minutes or until done. Remove from baking sheets; cool on racks. When cooled, frost points of star coffee cakes with Vanilla Frosting. Decorate alternate points with poinsettias made by cutting flowers and leaves from red and green candied cherries. Place pecan halves on remaining points. Makes 2 coffee cakes.

Vanilla Frosting: Combine 2½ c. sifted confectioners sugar, 2 tblsp. soft butter or regular margarine, 3 tblsp. milk and 1 tsp. vanilla in bowl; beat until smooth.

CHRISTMAS MORNING BRIOCHE

Surprise a neighbor Christmas morning with a napkin-lined basket filled with these lemon-flavored rolls

¼ c. milk	¼ c. lukewarm water
1 c. butter or regular	(110–115°)
margarine	6 eggs
½ c. sugar	4½ c. sifted flour
½ tsp. salt	1 egg white, slightly beaten
2 tsp. grated lemon rind	1 tblsp. water
2 pkgs. active dry yeast	

Heat milk and butter in saucepan over low heat until butter is melted. Pour over sugar, salt and lemon rind in mixing bowl. Cool to lukewarm.

Sprinkle yeast on ¼ c. lukewarm water; stir to dissolve. Add yeast, eggs and 3 c. flour to milk mixture. Beat with electric mixer at medium speed 4 minutes, scraping bowl occasionally.

Gradually stir in remaining flour, beating until smooth. Cover and let rise in warm place until doubled, about 1 hour. Stir down dough. Cover with aluminum foil. Refrigerate overnight.

Divide dough into 32 pieces. With floured hands, shape 24 of the pieces into balls. Place in 24 greased 3″ muffin-pan cups. Flatten and make an indentation in the center of each. Divide 8 remaining pieces into thirds, making 24 small pieces. Shape into teardrop shapes. Place in indentations, pointed side down. Cover and let rise until doubled, about 45 minutes. Brush with combined egg white and 1 tblsp. water.

Bake in 375° oven 12 to 15 minutes or until golden brown. Remove from pans. Delicious served warm. Makes 24.

REGAL SAVARIN RING

Even more luscious topped with puffs of whipped cream

1 pkg. active dry yeast	3 eggs
⅓ c. lukewarm water (110–115°)	2 tsp. grated orange rind
½ c. sifted flour	1¼ c. sifted flour
1 tblsp. sugar	¾ c. fresh orange juice
½ c. butter or regular margarine	½ c. water
½ c. sugar	⅔ c. sugar
½ tsp. salt	¾ c. warmed orange marmalade

Sprinkle yeast on ⅓ c. lukewarm water in small bowl; stir to dissolve. Stir in ½ c. flour and 1 tblsp. sugar. Cover and let stand in warm place until bubbly, about 1 hour.

Cream together butter, ½ c. sugar and salt in large bowl with electric mixer until light and fluffy. Add eggs, one at a time, beating well after each addition. Add yeast mixture, orange rind and 1¼ c. flour. Beat at medium speed of electric mixer 2 minutes. Turn mixture into well-greased 1½-qt. ring mold. Cover and let rise in warm place until doubled, about 1 hour.

Bake in 350° oven 35 minutes or until golden brown.

Meanwhile, combine orange juice, ½ c. water and ⅔ c. sugar in 2-qt. saucepan. Cook over medium heat, stirring constantly, until mixture comes to a boil. Remove from heat.

When bread tests done, remove from ring mold immediately. Place on cooling rack over waxed paper. Brush with hot orange syrup until it is all absorbed, about 15 minutes. Brush with orange marmalade. Makes 10 to 12 servings.

SUGARPLUM COFFEE RING

A festive coffee cake filled with swirls of melted sugar

½ c. milk, scalded	1 c. sugar
⅓ c. shortening	1¼ tsp. ground cinnamon
⅓ c. sugar	6 tblsp. melted butter or
1 tsp. salt	regular margarine
1 pkg. active dry yeast	½ c. toasted slivered
¼ c. lukewarm water	almonds
(110–115°)	½ c. quartered red candied
2 eggs	cherries
3¼ c. sifted flour	⅓ c. dark corn syrup

Combine milk, shortening, ⅓ c. sugar and salt in mixing bowl. Cool to lukewarm.

Sprinkle yeast on lukewarm water; stir to dissolve. Add yeast, eggs and 1 c. flour to milk mixture. Beat with electric mixer at medium speed 2 minutes, scraping bowl occasionally. Or beat with a spoon until batter is smooth. Gradually add enough flour to make a soft dough that leaves the sides of the bowl. Place in greased bowl. Cover and let rise until doubled, about 2 hours.

Punch down dough. Let rest 10 minutes. Turn dough out on floured surface. Divide in thirds. Cut each third into 12 parts; shape into balls.

Combine 1 c. sugar and cinnamon. Dip balls in melted butter and then in sugar-cinnamon mixture. Arrange 12 balls in greased 10″ tube pan with a solid bottom. (If your tube pan has a removable bottom, cover outside of pan with foil to prevent leaking.) Sprinkle with ⅓ of almonds and cherries. Repeat layers twice more.

Mix together corn syrup and remaining butter from dipping balls. Drizzle on top. Cover and let rise until doubled, about 1 hour.

Bake in 350° oven 35 minutes or until done. Cool in pan on rack 5 minutes. Remove from pan. Serve warm, top side up. Makes 12 servings.

MARASCHINO CHERRY LOAVES

An Indiana woman created this recipe for her children because they were getting tired of plain white bread

1 c. milk
¾ c. water
2 tblsp. shortening
2 tblsp. sugar
2 tsp. salt
1 pkg. active dry yeast
¼ c. lukewarm water
   (110–115°)

6 to 6½ c. sifted flour
½ c. chopped red
   maraschino cherries
Confectioners Sugar Icing
   (recipe follows)

Heat milk and ¾ c. water in small saucepan to scalding. Pour over shortening, sugar and salt in mixing bowl. Cool to lukewarm.

Sprinkle yeast over ¼ c. lukewarm water; stir to dissolve.

Add yeast mixture and 2 c. flour to milk mixture. Beat with electric mixer at medium speed, about 2 minutes, scraping bowl occasionally. Or beat with spoon until batter is smooth.

Gradually stir in enough flour to make a soft dough that leaves the sides of the bowl. Stir in maraschino cherries. Turn dough out on floured surface and knead until smooth and satiny, about 15 minutes.

Place dough in lightly greased bowl; turn over to grease top. Cover and let rise in warm place until doubled, about 1 hour.

Punch down dough. Divide dough in half. Shape each half into loaf and place in greased 9×5×3″ loaf pan. Cover and let rise until doubled, about 1 hour.

Bake in 350° oven 40 minutes or until breads test done. Remove from pans; cool on racks. Frost with Confectioners Sugar Icing. Makes 2 loaves.

Confectioners Sugar Icing: Combine 1 c. sifted confectioners sugar, 1 tblsp. milk and 1 tsp. vanilla in bowl; beat until smooth.

FESTIVE CRANBERRY LOAF

Wrap in plastic wrap and tie with a big red ribbon. Attach a few small Christmas ornaments or sprigs of holly

2 c. sifted flour	**¾ c. fresh orange juice**
1 c. sugar	**1 tblsp. grated orange rind**
1½ tsp. baking powder	**1 c. coarsely chopped**
1 tsp. salt	**cranberries**
½ tsp. baking soda	**¼ c. chopped walnuts**
¼ c. shortening	**1 tblsp. flour**
1 egg, beaten	

Sift together 2 c. flour, sugar, baking powder, salt and baking soda into mixing bowl.

Cut in shortening with pastry blender or two knives until mixture is crumbly. Combine egg, orange juice and orange rind in small bowl. Add to crumb mixture all at once, stirring just enough to moisten.

Combine cranberries, walnuts and 1 tblsp. flour. Stir into batter. Pour batter into greased and waxed paper-lined 8½ ×4½ ×2½″ loaf pan.

Bake in 350° oven 1 hour or until bread tests done. Remove from pan; cool on rack. Wrap loaf in aluminum foil. Let stand overnight for easier slicing. Makes 1 loaf.

CHRISTMAS FRUIT/NUT LOAF

One farm woman's friends look forward to this homemade bread every year

2 c. sifted flour	1 tblsp. grated orange rind
1 c. sugar	1 egg, beaten
1½ tsp. baking powder	1½ c. chopped fresh or
½ tsp. baking soda	frozen cranberries
1 tsp. salt	½ c. chopped walnuts
¼ c. shortening	½ c. cut-up candied orange
1 c. orange juice	slices

Sift together flour, sugar, baking powder, baking soda and salt into mixing bowl. Cut in shortening with pastry blender or two knives until mixture resembles coarse cornmeal. Add orange juice, orange rind and egg; mix just enough to moisten. Stir in cranberries, walnuts and orange slices. Pour batter into greased 9×5×3″ loaf pan.

Bake in 350° oven 1 hour or until golden brown. Cool in pan on rack 5 minutes. Remove from pan; cool on rack. Wrap loaf in aluminum foil and let stand 24 hours for easier slicing. Makes 1 loaf.

GLORIOUS GOLDEN FRUITCAKE

Fruitcake lovers will like this light cake for a change

4 c. sifted flour	½ c. chopped candied
1½ tsp. baking powder	pineapple
½ tsp. salt	½ c. chopped red candied
2 c. butter or regular	cherries
margarine	½ c. chopped green candied
2½ c. sugar	cherries
6 eggs	1 tblsp. grated lemon rind
¼ c. milk	Pineapple Glaze (recipe
4 c. chopped walnuts	follows)
1 c. golden raisins	Pecan halves

Sift together flour, baking powder and salt; reserve ¼ c. of flour mixture.

Cream together butter and sugar until light and fluffy, using electric mixer at medium speed. Add eggs, one at a time, beating well. Add dry ingredients alternately with milk, beating well after each addition.

Combine walnuts, raisins, pineapple, candied red and green cherries, lemon rind and ¼ c. reserved flour mixture. Stir into batter. Spread batter in greased and waxed paper-lined 10″ tube pan.

Bake in 275° oven 2 hours 45 minutes or until done. Cool in pan 30 minutes. Remove from pan; cool on rack.

Wrap fruitcake tightly in foil. Store in refrigerator up to 4 weeks. (Fruitcake keeps better if stored unfrosted.)

To serve: Prepare Pineapple Glaze. Frost top of cake, letting glaze drip down sides. Decorate with pecan halves. Makes 1 (5 lb.) fruitcake.

Pineapple Glaze: Combine 1 c. sifted confectioners sugar and 2 tblsp. pineapple juice; mix until smooth.

CHRISTMAS SNOW CAKE

Whether you have snow or not, celebrate a white Christmas with this lovely angel food swirled with lots of whipped cream

1 (10″) angel food cake
3 c. heavy cream
½ tsp. rum flavoring
¼ c. chopped candied red
    cherries
¼ c. chopped candied green
    cherries

¼ c. raisins
¼ c. chopped pecans
1⅓ c. flaked coconut
Candied red and green
    cherries, cut up

Cut cake into 3 horizontal layers.

Whip cream and rum flavoring in mixing bowl until thick, using electric mixer at high speed. Remove 1 c. whipped cream. Fold in ¼ c. red and ¼ c. green cherries. Remove 1 more cup of whipped cream. Fold in raisins and pecans.

Place bottom layer of cake on serving plate. Spread with raisin filling. Top with middle layer. Spread with candied cherry filling. Top with third layer of cake. Frost sides and top of cake with remaining whipped cream. Decorate sides and top of cake with coconut. Decorate top of cake with cut-up red and green cherries. Refrigerate until serving time. Makes 12 servings.

GLAZED FRUIT GÂTEAU

Reminiscent of European-type cakes that are so beautiful. Filled with custard filling

2 (9") round yellow cake
   layers
1 (3¼ oz.) pkg. lemon
   pudding and pie filling
1½ tsp. grated lemon rind
1 (1 lb. 13 oz.) can pear
   halves, drained
1 (8¾ oz.) can apricot
   halves, drained

14 red maraschino cherries,
   halved
¾ c. peach or apricot
   preserves
1 c. heavy cream
1 tblsp. sugar
1 tsp. vanilla
1 drop yellow food color
½ c. toasted sliced almonds

Cut cake layers in half horizontally, making 4 layers.

Prepare lemon pudding and pie filling according to package directions. Remove from heat. Stir in lemon rind. Cool well.

Reserve 4 pear halves, 5 apricot halves and 8 maraschino cherry halves; set aside. Chop remaining fruit and fold into cooled custard filling.

Spread filling between layers. On top of cake, arrange reserved pears and apricots in a symmetrical deisgn, cut side down. Place cherries on sides of pears.

Melt preserves in saucepan over low heat. Press through sieve. Spoon quickly over fruit.

Whip cream in bowl using electric mixer at high speed until thickened. Add sugar, vanilla and food color. Beat until soft peaks form. Reserve ½ c.; frost cake with remaining cream. Stud sides of cake with almonds.

Using rosette decorating tip and reserved ½ c. cream, pipe a border around top edge of cake. Refrigerate until serving time. Makes 12 servings.

FESTIVE HOLIDAY DESSERT

Sprinkle cake with a little brandy or sherry if you like before assembling the trifle

5 eggs
¾ c. sugar
½ tsp. almond flavoring
¾ c. sifted cake flour
¾ tsp. baking powder
¼ tsp. salt
1 (4¾ oz.) pkg. vanilla
  pudding and pie filling
3¾ c. milk
1½ tsp. vanilla
2 (10 oz.) pkgs. frozen
  raspberries, thawed

¼ c. sugar
2 tblsp. cornstarch
1 tblsp. lemon juice
1 (1 lb. 13 oz.) can sliced
  peaches, well drained
1⅓ c. flaked coconut
1 pt. heavy cream
¼ c. sugar
1 tsp. vanilla
Toasted slivered almonds
3 red maraschino cherries
  with stems

Combine eggs, ¾ c. sugar and almond flavoring in mixing bowl. Beat with electric mixer at high speed until thick and lemon-colored, about 5 minutes.

Sift together cake flour, baking powder and salt. Fold dry ingredients into egg mixture. Spread batter in well-greased 15½ × 10½ × 1″ jelly roll pan.

Bake in 350° oven 20 minutes or until cake tests done. Loosen cake around edges. Turn out on rack to cool.

Combine pudding and milk in 2-qt. saucepan. Cook over medium heat, stirring constantly, until mixture comes to a boil. Remove from heat. Pour into a metal bowl; place in iced water. Stir with rubber spatula until mixture is room temperature. Add 1½ tsp. vanilla. Set aside.

Drain raspberries, reserving liquid. Add enough water to raspberry liquid to make 1½ c. Combine ¼ c. sugar and cornstarch in 2-qt. saucepan. Gradually stir in reserved 1½ c. liquid and lemon juice. Cook over medium heat, stirring constantly, until thickened. Remove from heat; stir in raspberries. Cool well.

Divide cake into thirds. Tear each third into small pieces. Layer ⅓ of cake in 4-qt. crystal bowl. Top with ⅓ of raspberry sauce, ½ of peaches, ½ of coconut and ⅓ of custard. Repeat layers. Top with remaining cake, raspberries and custard. Refrigerate at least 1 hour.

Whip cream in bowl until it begins to thicken, using electric mixer at high speed. Beat in ¼ c. sugar and 1 tsp. vanilla. Swirl over top of dessert. Decorate with almonds and maraschino cherries. Makes 12 servings.

AMBROSIA DESSERT BOWL

Make this super dessert ahead and refrigerate overnight

20 large marshmallows	1 (8¼ oz.) can crushed
3 c. heavy cream	pineapple, well drained
2 tblsp. sugar	1 c. flaked coconut
¼ tsp. salt	3 c. pound cake cubes (1″)
2 tsp. vanilla	6 large oranges, peeled and
½ tsp. almond flavoring	cut in sections

Combine marshmallows and ¼ c. of the heavy cream in top of double boiler. Heat over boiling water until marshmallows are melted. Remove from heat. Cool.

Whip remaining 2¾ c. heavy cream with sugar until it is thick and creamy. Fold whipped cream into marshmallow mixture. Fold in salt, vanilla, almond flavoring, pineapple and coconut.

Layer ½ of cake cubes in 2-qt. crystal bowl. Top with ½ of oranges and ½ of filling. Repeat layers. Cover and chill in refrigerator several hours or overnight. Makes 8 to 10 servings.

TANGY CRANBERRY CONSERVE

Spoon into a crystal serving dish for two gifts in one

2 c. fresh or frozen whole
   cranberries
½ c. sugar

2 c. prepared mincemeat
1 tsp. grated orange rind

Combine cranberries, sugar, mincemeat and orange rind in saucepan. Bring mixture to a boil; reduce heat. Simmer 10 minutes or until cranberries are tender, stirring occasionally.

Remove from heat; cool well. Store mixture in covered container in refrigerator. Makes 2 cups.

HOLIDAY CRANBERRY RELISH

Spoon into orange or lemon shells to garnish the holiday ham

1 lb. whole cranberries,
   fresh or frozen
5 medium apples

2 medium oranges
2 c. sugar

Grind cranberries, apples and oranges in food grinder, using medium blade. Place mixture in bowl. Stir in sugar; mix until sugar is dissolved. Spoon into 1-pint freezer containers. Cover and freeze. Thaw slightly before serving. Makes 4 pints.

Chapter 9

HOW TO CREATE YOUR OWN CONTAINERS FOR FOOD GIFTS

Part of the pleasure of giving food gifts is developing new ways to present them. And so we present some eye-catching containers that will last long after the food has been demolished. This chapter provides step-by-step instructions on an assortment of containers that are fun to make and charming to give. Some are very simple to make while others do take a bit more expertise.

Take an oatmeal box and turn it into a Pink Elephant Gift Box to delight a child. Or make a Toy Train from empty quart milk cartons. Save half-pint milk cartons and make the Half-pint Mouse.

A recycled olive jar can be transformed into a Cheerful Butterfly Jar to hold a relish or jam.

We have several gift boxes to make if you don't have much time to spend or if you need a container at the last minute. They look very special even though they don't take long to make.

After you have tried all of the ideas in this chapter, you might create your own original containers using these as springboard ideas.

We give food suggestions for every gift package. They range from containers to hold rolls, candy and cookies to a sew-it-yourself holder for casseroles.

GENERAL DIRECTIONS

How to enlarge patterns: If pattern is shown on a grid, rule paper with 1″ squares and copy the pattern outline from the smaller squares to the corresponding large squares, using the squares as a drawing guide (see Figure 1).

Making circles: Use a compass to trace circles on colored paper. If you don't have a compass, see directions with Casserole Carrier for making a string compass, or use small cans, bottles and coins for patterns.

Paper: Package decorations are cut from construction paper, gift wrap, self-adhesive plastic, colored tissue papers and thin white paper called layout paper, available at art supply stores. You can use typing paper, but the layout paper comes in larger sizes, in tablets.

Glue: Ordinary white glue can be used for package designs made from construction paper or gift wrap. But white glue causes colored tissue paper and ribbon to bleed and pucker—rubber cement is a better choice for these materials.

Figure 1: HOW TO ENLARGE PATTERNS

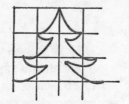

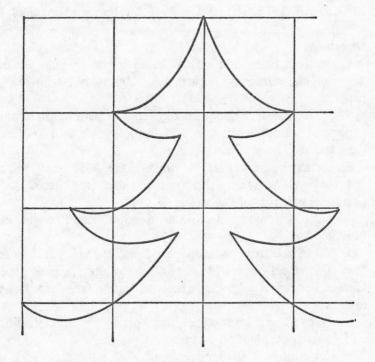

TOY TRAIN

For color photo, see Plate 1

Materials:

4 (1 qt.) milk cartons
3 (12×9″) sheets orange
    construction paper
1 (9×6″) sheet white
    construction paper

2 (12×9″) sheets yellow
    construction paper
1 (9×6″) sheet bright pink
    construction paper
12″ yellow cord or ribbon

Directions:

1. Cut tops from milk cartons, making one 6″ high, for engine cab; the remaining 3 cars, 4½″ high. Cover with orange paper.

2. To complete engine, enlarge engine pattern on orange paper and cut out. Form into cylinder; glue, fold tabs to center. Glue tabs to cab (see Step 1).

3. For engine front, cut 3½″ white circle, 2½″ orange circle and 1¼″ yellow circle. Glue them together (see Step 2) and glue to tabs at front of engine.

4. Trace pattern and cut 8 train windows. Glue to engine cab (see Step 3).

5. Cut wheels from yellow paper: 8 circles 2½″ and 2 circles 3¼″. Cut wheel centers (1¼″ circles) from bright pink paper. Glue centers to wheels; glue wheels to engine (see Step 3) and to cars.

6. Trace pattern for roof on yellow paper, placing dotted line on fold. Cut out; place on engine.

7. Cut cord in 3 (4″) pieces. Cut X's near bottom of train cars; hook cars together through X's and knot. Fill train with candies and cookies.

TOY TRAIN

TRAIN WINDOW

Actual Size 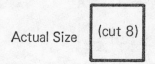 (cut 8)

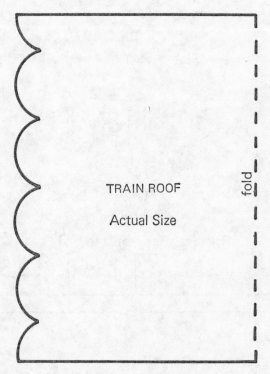

TRAIN ROOF

Actual Size

fold

(1/2 of roof pattern.
Place dotted line on
fold of paper and trace)

TOY TRAIN

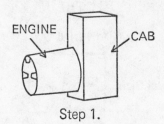

ENGINE CAB

Step 1.

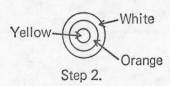

Yellow — White

Orange

Step 2.

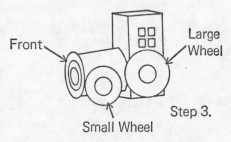

Front — Large Wheel

Small Wheel

Step 3.

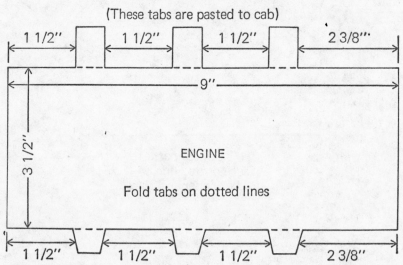

(These tabs are pasted to cab)

1 1/2"   1 1/2"   1 1/2"   2 3/8"'

9"

3 1/2"

ENGINE

Fold tabs on dotted lines

1 1/2"   1 1/2"   1 1/2"   2 3/8"

PINK ELEPHANT GIFT BOX

For color photo, see Plate 4

Materials:

1 (1 lb. 2 oz.) oatmeal box
Bright pink construction
  paper
White construction paper
Orange construction paper

Yellow construction paper
6″ yellow cord
4 corks
White tempera paint

Directions:

You need pink paper 13″ long to wrap oatmeal cartons. If your construction paper is not this big, glue pieces together as necessary to make size specified. Note that the lid is covered separately so it can be removed to get at the goodies.

1. Cut pink paper 13×6½″ and glue to oatmeal box, overlapping seams.

2. On pink paper, trace 2 circles, using lid as pattern. Cut out. Glue 1 circle to bottom of box; glue other circle to lid. Cut pink strip (13×¾″) and glue around rim of lid.

3. Trace elephant ears, mouth and eyes on white paper; cut out. Cut elephant inner ears from yellow paper; glue inner ears to ears. Glue eyes, mouth and ears to *bottom* of oatmeal box, making elephant face.

4. Trace trunk on pink paper; cut out; fold and staple end as shown in Step 1 and glue trunk to face (see Step 2).

5. Cut an X in center of lid; push cord through and knot, to make tail.

6. Paint 4 corks white; glue to body of elephant.

7. Place plastic bag inside box. Fill with candies or cookies. Close with twist-tie. Place tail on elephant.

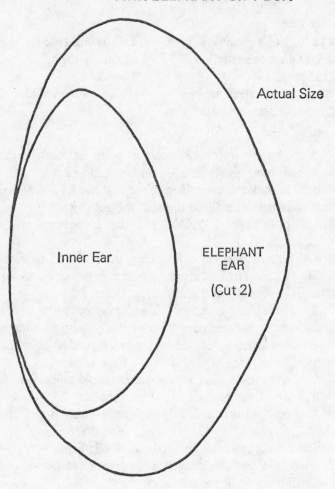

PINK ELEPHANT GIFT BOX

Actual Size

Inner Ear

ELEPHANT
EAR

(Cut 2)

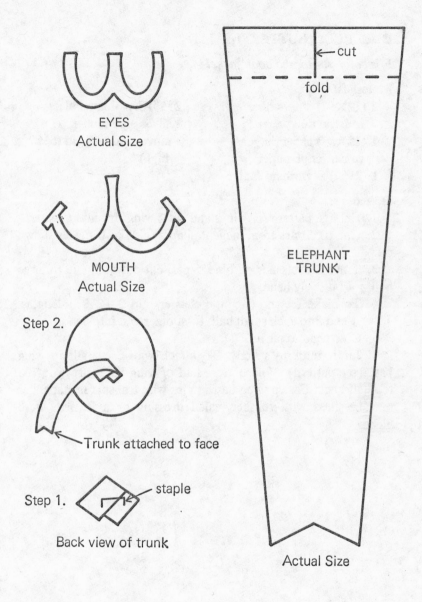

EYES
Actual Size

MOUTH
Actual Size

Step 2.

Trunk attached to face

Step 1.

staple

Back view of trunk

ELEPHANT
TRUNK

cut

fold

Actual Size

CHEERFUL BUTTERFLY JAR

For color photo, see book jacket

Materials:

2 (12×9″) sheets blue
    construction paper
1 (12×9″) sheet magenta
    construction paper
1 (2½″) Styrofoam ball

2 (1″) Styrofoam balls
1 silver pipe cleaner
1 narrow jar with lid (5½″
    high)

Directions:

1. Enlarge pattern for wings and cut 2 wings from blue paper.

2. Cut 10 circles from magenta paper; glue to wings as shown on pattern.

3. Trace 2 eyelashes on blue paper; cut out and glue to large ball, for butterfly head.

4. To make feelers, cut pipe cleaner into 2 (2½″) lengths. Twist 1 end into each small ball; twist other end into head.

5. Glue head to jar lid.

6. Jar is butterfly's body. To attach wings, cut slit in wing base (see pattern). Fold bottom half of wing base forward; fold top half back. Fasten wing bases to jar with transparent tape. Jar may be filled with relishes, salad dressing or a favorite herb blend.

CHEERFUL BUTTERFLY JAR

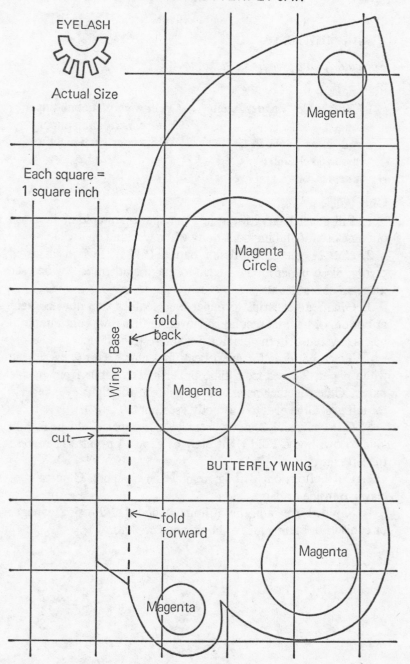

EYELASH

Actual Size

Each square = 1 square inch

Magenta

Magenta Circle

Wing Base

fold back

Magenta

cut →

BUTTERFLY WING

fold forward

Magenta

Magenta

TISSUE OWL BAG

For color photo, see book jacket

Materials:

1 (10½×5½″) paper lunch bag

1 roll tissue paper in assorted colors, (we used purples, blues and greens)

Yellow construction paper

Blue construction paper

White construction paper

Directions:

1. Fill paper bag with crushed newspapers; staple or tape top of bag closed. (Stuffing adds body when working on owl.)

2. Cut 21 pieces of tissue paper 16½×2½″ in assorted colors. Slash paper along 1 edge to make feathers ½″ wide (see diagram of feather strip).

3. Glue feather strips to paper bag, feather side down. Begin at bottom of bag; let second row overlap first row; continue until bag is covered. Alternate colors for interesting effect.

4. Trace patterns for eyes, beak and claws. Cut 2 eyes from white paper, 2 irises from blue paper and 2 pupils from purple paper. Glue together as shown on pattern for right eye; reverse for left eye. Glue eyes to owl body (see photo).

5. Cut beak and 2 claws from yellow paper. Fold beak and glue to owl body. Fold right claw as shown on pattern; reverse for left claw.

6. Cut bottom out of bag; remove newspapers. Glue tabs of claws to inside of bag.

7. Slip owl over a bottle of homemade salad dressing, vinegar or canister of baking mix or homemade cookies.

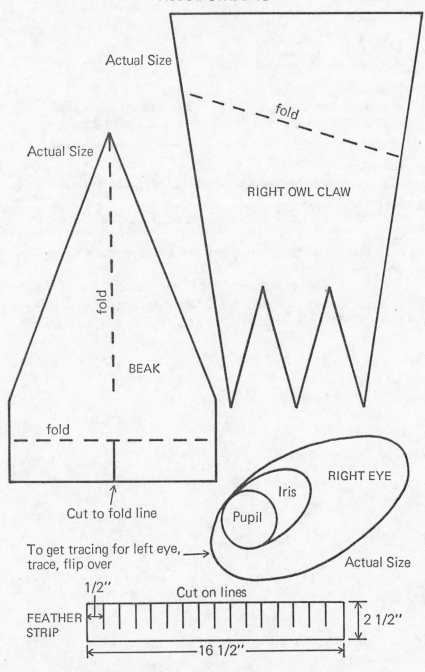

TISSUE OWL BAG

Actual Size

fold

RIGHT OWL CLAW

Actual Size

fold

BEAK

fold

Cut to fold line

RIGHT EYE

Iris

Pupil

To get tracing for left eye, trace, flip over

Actual Size

1/2"

Cut on lines

FEATHER STRIP

2 1/2"

16 1/2"

HAPPY SUN PLATE

For color photo, see book jacket

Materials:

Red construction paper	1 (9″) yellow paper plate
9″ red bulky yarn	1 (12 oz.) salad dressing bottle

Directions:

1. Trace patterns for nose, eyelashes and mouth corners on red paper; cut out.

2. Glue yarn smile on plate face, covering ends with mouth corners.

3. Fold nose and glue to plate; fold eyelashes and glue above nose.

4. Cut 1 piece red paper 7½ ×2″ and glue to back of plate to make a loop (see Figure 1). Slip loop over salad dressing bottle filled with homemade salad dressing.

HAPPY SUN PLATE

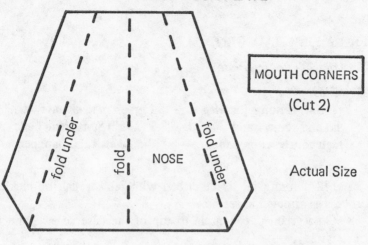

fold under

fold

NOSE

fold under

MOUTH CORNERS
(Cut 2)

Actual Size

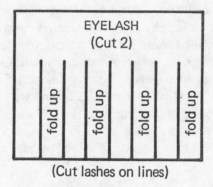

EYELASH
(Cut 2)

fold up

fold up

fold up

fold up

(Cut lashes on lines)

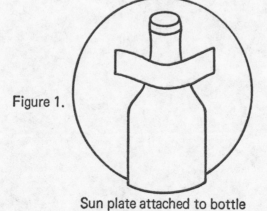

Figure 1.

Sun plate attached to bottle

FROG PINT JAR GIFT

For color photo, see Plate 7

Materials:

1 (1 pint) canning jar with lid and screw band
Green construction paper

1 green pipe cleaner
2 (1½″) Styrofoam balls
Blue construction paper

Directions:

1. Fill canning jar as described with jelly, relish or pickles. Process as directed in recipe.

2. Glue green paper circle to top of jar (use screw band to trace circle).

3. To make eyes, cut 2 (3″) lengths from green pipe cleaner. Wrap around center of balls. Glue eyes to covered lid.

4. Trace patterns for frog arms on green paper. Enlarge leg pattern and trace on green paper. Cut out; fold on dotted line.

5. From blue paper, cut out different-size spots in irregular shapes (no pattern needed). Glue spots to arms and legs. Tape arms and legs to canning jar.

FROG PINT JAR GIFT
Actual Size

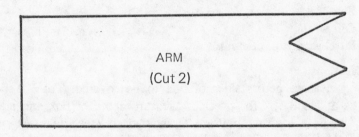

ARM
(Cut 2)

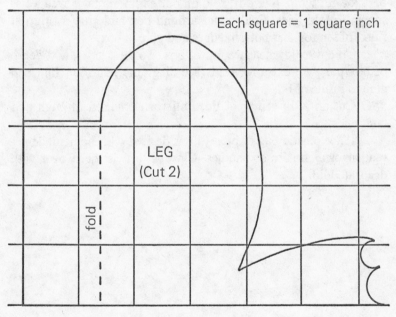

Each square = 1 square inch

LEG
(Cut 2)

fold

YARN POMPON GIFT BOX

For color photo, see Plate 7

Materials:
  Box of desired size
  Gift wrap
  Purchased yarn pompon

Directions:

1. Measure across sides of box to be covered. Total the 4 sides and add ½″ for overlap. Measure depth of box and add ¾″ at both top and bottom. Draw pattern (see diagram) on back of gift wrap. Cut out; fold on dotted lines; cut V wedges as shown to fold lines. Fold paper around box and glue overlap at side; fold in top and bottom edges and glue to box.

2. To cover lid, measure top of box. To all 4 sides, add depth of box plus ¾″ extra for fold (see diagram). Cut out, fold and glue to inside of lid.

3. Cut an X in center of lid. Pull yarn pompon through and knot ends.

4. Place plastic bag in box. Fill as desired with homemade cereal snacks, cookies or candies. Close with twist-tie. Cover with decorated lid.

YARN POMPON GIFT BOX

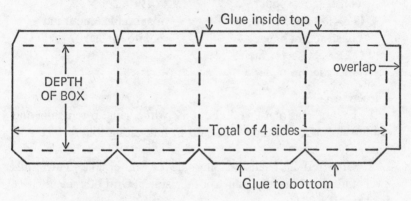

Glue inside top

DEPTH OF BOX

overlap →

Total of 4 sides

Glue to bottom

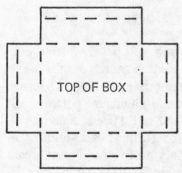

TOP OF BOX

SAILBOAT BIRTHDAY CUPCAKES

For color photo, see book jacket

Materials:

4 (12×9″) sheets white construction paper

2 (12×9″) sheets red construction paper

2 (12×9″) sheets blue construction paper

12 plastic drinking straws

12 (4¼×2⅜×⅞″) disposable aluminum potato shells

Directions:

1. Enlarge sail pattern and cut 12 white sails, 6 red sails and 6 blue sails. Cut red and blue sails in half along line A (see pattern).

2. Glue red half-sails to one side of white sails. Turn sails over and glue blue half-sail to other side. (On both sides, color is at right.)

3. Glue straw to sail along line A, letting straw extend about ½″ above top of sail.

4. Trace pattern for flag; cut 6 from red paper, 6 from blue paper. Slit flags on line and insert into straws at top of sails.

5. Prepare 1 (1 lb. 2½ oz.) cake mix according to package directions. Pour batter into 12 greased aluminum potato shells placed on baking sheet, filling one-half full. (Use remaining batter for cupcakes.) Bake in 350° oven 18 minutes or until cakes test done. Cool on racks. Frost with your favorite butter cream frosting. (You will need approximately 1 c. frosting for 12 sailboats.) Insert sails into frosted cakes. Makes 12.

SAILBOAT BIRTHDAY CUPCAKES

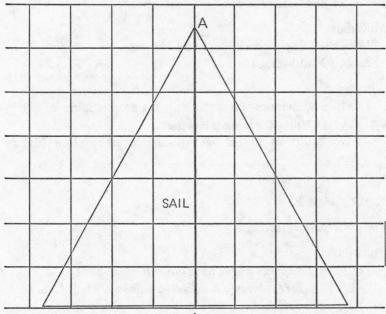

A

SAIL

A

Each square = 1 square inch

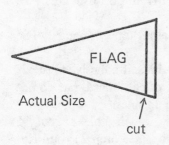

FLAG

Actual Size

cut

BIRTHDAY PARTY FAVORS

For color photo, see Plate 7

Materials:
   12 colored disposable aluminum tart pans
   Assorted yarn scraps

Directions:
   1. Fill 6 aluminum tart pans with assorted candies or other treats; cover with remaining 6 tart pans.
   2. Tie yarn bows around pans to hold covers in place. Makes 6 favors.

ROLL BASKET

For color photo, see Plate 1

Materials:
   1 (12" square) sheet poster board or thin cardboard
   2 (12½" square) pieces self-adhesive plastic, such as Con-Tact
   2 yds. (½") ribbon

Directions:
   1. Cut bottom and 4 sides for basket from poster board. (see Step 1 for sizes).
   2. Tape sides to bottom with transparent tape, leaving 1/16" space between pieces as illustrated.
   3. Cover both sides of poster board with self-adhesive plastic.
   4. Trim plastic cover even with edge of cardboard, but do not cut away corners—leave it square. Fold up sides.
   5. Cut ribbon in 4 (18") lengths. Punch hole or cut X through plastic flap at each corner of box (see Step 2); pull ribbon through holes; tie bows. Fill with rolls, candies, cookies or cake squares.

ROLL BASKET

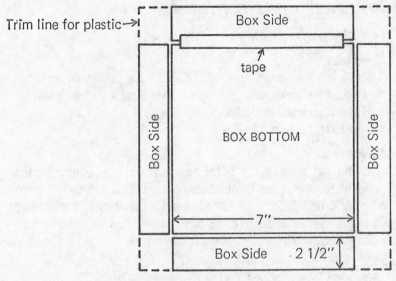

Trim line for plastic →

Box Side

tape

Box Side

BOX BOTTOM

Box Side

7"

Box Side   2 1/2"

Step 1.

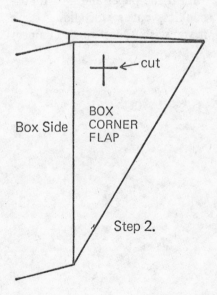

← cut

Box Side

BOX
CORNER
FLAP

Step 2.

DECORATED PINT CONTAINER

For color photo, see Plate 7

Materials:

2 (1 pint) ice cream containers with lids	Matching tissue paper
Gift wrap or self-adhesive plastic, such as Con-Tact	Matching bow (optional)

Directions:

1. To get pattern for covering an ice cream container that flares at the top, take 1 container apart. Lay it flat on gift paper or plastic and trace outline, adding ¼" to 1 side for overlap. Cut out. (Save pattern to cover other containers.)

2. Wrap paper around second ice cream container, overlapping seams. Glue in place.

3. Cover center of lid with matching paper.

4. Line decorated container with tissue paper and fill with assorted wrapped candies or cookies; cover with lid. Attach matching bow to center of lid, if you wish. Quart-size containers can also be used.

HALF-PINT MOUSE

For color photo, see book jacket

Materials:

1 (½ pint) milk carton
2 (12×9″) sheets light
   brown construction paper
Yellow construction paper
1 dark blue pipe cleaner

1 thumbtack
2 blue signal dots (or dots
   cut from blue paper)
8½″ yellow cord or yarn

Directions:

1. Unfold top of milk carton to make container 4″ high. Cover with brown paper.

2. On second sheet of brown paper, draw 1 (3½″) circle for face, and 2 (3″) circles for ears. On yellow paper, draw 2 (1¼″) circles for inner ears. Cut out. Glue inner ears to ears.

3. Cut blue pipe cleaner in half. Bend each length into V, for whiskers. Glue to face, with a thumbtack nose in the center.

4. Glue ¼″ round blue eyes to face; glue ears to face; glue face to carton.

5. Cut an X in center back of carton, near bottom. Insert yellow cord and knot for tail. Fill carton with wrapped candies or cookies.

TISSUE BOX HOUSE

For color photo, see Plate 7

Materials:

Poster board or heavy white
　paper
2 (12×9") sheets purple
　construction paper
1 (9×6") sheet gold
　construction paper

1 decorator tissue box,
　about 5" high
1 gold thumbtack

Directions:

1. Cut roof (9½×7") from poster board; fold in half (see Step 1).

2. Cut 5 purple strips and 5 gold strips to decorate roof, each 7×1⅛". Beginning at bottom edge of roof, glue strips to roof, alternating colors and overlapping strips ⅛".

3. Trace pattern for roof support; cut 2 from poster board and 2 from purple paper. Glue purple paper to poster board; fold on dotted lines and glue supports (purple side out) to underside of roof, leaving an overhang of 1¼" (see Step 2).

4. Cut 2 pieces of purple paper 9×5" to cover tissue box. Glue in place.

5. Trace pattern for door and draw 8 windows (1"×1") on gold paper; cut out and glue to sides of house. (See Figure 1 for window arrangement.) For doorknob, use a gold thumbtack.

6. Fill box house with cookies, candies, confections or a mix, tied in plastic bag. Lay roof over top.

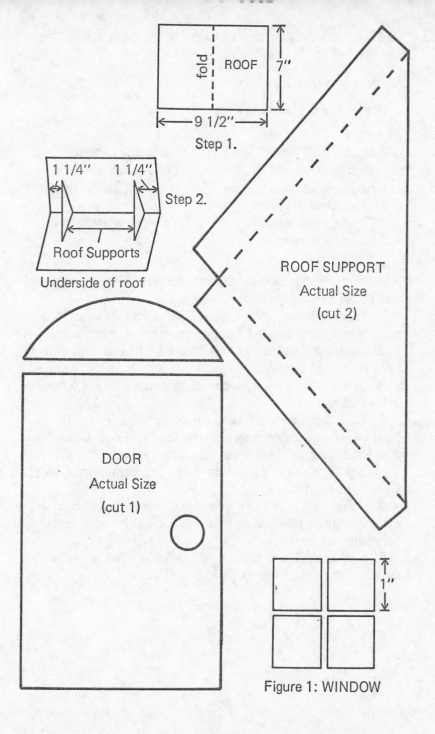

fold ROOF

7''

← 9 1/2'' →

Step 1.

1 1/4'' 1 1/4''

Step 2.

Roof Supports

Underside of roof

ROOF SUPPORT
Actual Size
(cut 2)

DOOR
Actual Size
(cut 1)

1''

Figure 1: WINDOW

MAN IN TOP HAT BOX

For color photo, see book jacket

Materials:

1 (8×4¼×3″) white box with lid
Orange construction paper
Pink construction paper
18″ orange bulky yarn
1 orange pipe cleaner

1 black pipe cleaner
2 (½″) glitter trim eyes
1 (18×7½″) piece red print fabric
Blue construction paper

Directions:

If you have a long box, decorate lid with a funny face and stand it on end.

1. Trace hair pattern on orange paper; cut 2. Enlarge nose pattern and cut pink nose. Loop orange yarn to make mustache; fasten with orange pipe cleaner or thread. Cut eyebrows 1″ long from black pipe cleaner.

2. Glue eyebrows, eyes, nose and mustache to lid of box; glue hair to sides of lid.

3. To stiffen fabric necktie, cut paper slightly smaller than fabric. Lay paper on wrong side of fabric and fold like a business letter, fabric right side out (see Step 1). Fold ends to center (see Step 2); pinch to make bow shape and staple (see Step 3). Glue tie under face.

4. To make top hat, cut blue paper 12×3½″ and form into cylinder; glue edge. Cut 6½″ circle for hat brim; glue hat to brim; glue hat to box.

5. Line box with aluminum foil; fill with cookies, brownies, doughnuts or rolls. Cover with decorated lid.

MAN IN TOP HAT BOX

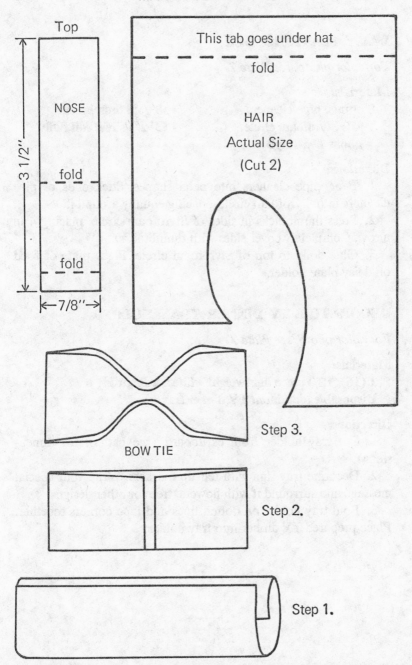

Top

NOSE

fold

fold

3 1/2"

7/8"

This tab goes under hat

fold

HAIR
Actual Size
(Cut 2)

BOW TIE

Step 3.

Step 2.

Step 1.

DAISY PLATE HOLDER

For color photo, see Plate 7

Materials:

    8 orange pipe cleaners   135 gold thumbtacks
    1 (4″) Styrofoam circle,   1 (3½″) silver foil doily
      about 1½″ high

Directions:

1. Bend pipe cleaners into petal shapes. Stick ends of pipe cleaners into Styrofoam circle, spacing equally around it.

2. Press thumbtacks in sides of Styrofoam circle, placing 4 in a row. Completely cover sides with thumbtacks.

3. Glue doily to top of Styrofoam circle. Place plate of food on daisy plate holder.

DECORATIVE TV DINNER TRAY HOLDER

For color photo, see Plate 7

Materials:

    1 (16×12″) piece lightweight white cardboard
    Disposable aluminum TV dinner tray

Directions:

1. Cut tray holder from cardboard (see pattern for dimensions).

2. Decorate tray sign with felt-tip markers. Write your special message and surround it with flowers, trees or other designs.

3. Fold tray holder on dotted lines and tape corners together. Place prepared TV dinner into tray holder.

DECORATIVE TV DINNER TRAY

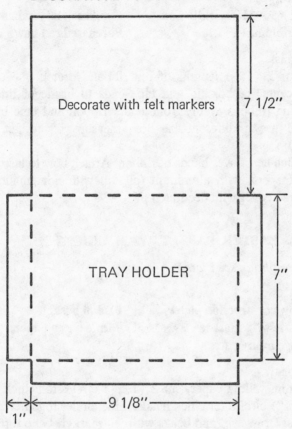

Decorate with felt markers

7 1/2"

TRAY HOLDER

7"

9 1/8"

1"

VALENTINE HEART BOX

For color photo, see Plate 7

Materials:

1 (11×9×2¼″) white box   Purchased 8″ red heart
Red ribbon, ½″ wide   Purchased red bow

Directions:

1. Cut 5 (15″) lengths of red ribbon. Stretch one of them across center of box lid and tape ends to inside of lid. Space remaining ribbons evenly from center ribbon and tape in place. (If you use a different-size box, measure lid to get ribbon length.)

2. Glue heart over bands of ribbon. Attach bow to heart.

3. Line box with aluminum foil; fill with homemade baked goods and cover with decorated lid.

SMALL EASTER BASKET WITH CHICKS

For color photo, see Plate 7

Materials:

Yellow construction paper   1 small basket
Black felt-tip marker   Purple tissue paper
Orange bulky yarn

Directions:

1. From yellow paper, cut 2 (1½″) circles for chick bodies, and 2 (1″) circles for chick heads. Glue circles together, making 2 chicks. Draw eyes and beaks with felt marker. Glue tufts of orange yarn to back of heads.

2. Tape chicks to basket so they peek out. Glue yarn around top edge of basket; tie yarn bow to handle.

3. Line basket with purple tissue paper and fill with assorted candies or other treats.

HALLOWEEN GHOST PARTY FAVOR

For color photo, see Plate 7

Materials:

1 drinking straw

1 (2") Styrofoam ball

1 white dinner-size paper
   napkin

24" orange bulky yarn

Black construction paper

1 (10 oz.) Styrofoam or clear
   plastic cup

Directions:

1. Insert straw in Styrofoam ball.

2. Cover ball with napkin and tie orange yarn bow around neck.

3. Trace pattern for eyes and mouth on black paper; cut out and glue to face.

4. Fill cup with candies or other goodies. Insert straw into cup.

HALLOWEEN GHOST PARTY FAVOR

EYES

Actual Size

MOUTH

WHITE CHRISTMAS TREE

For color photo, see Plate 4

Materials:

5 (17×14″) sheets thin
white paper, such as
layout paper from art
supply store

1 pack blue sequin flowers
Yellow construction paper
1 (12″) Styrofoam cone

Directions:

1. Cut 19 pieces of white paper, 13×3½″. Slash paper along 1 edge into strips ½″ wide (see diagram). Curl strips with edge of scissors, curling strips on 12 papers into tight curls and the remaining 7 into loose curls.

2. Coat uncut edge of paper with rubber cement. Starting at top of tree, wind curled paper around cone in spiral rows. Use tightly curled paper first, to cover upper part of tree; place curled edge up. Space rows as close as curls permit, to make tree full. Use loose curls on lower part.

3. Cut star from yellow paper. Glue to top of tree.

4. Glue blue sequin flowers to tree; place 1 in center of star.

5. Use tree to decorate a large gift box filled with homemade goodies. The recipient can then use the tree as a centerpiece.

WHITE CHRISTMAS TREE

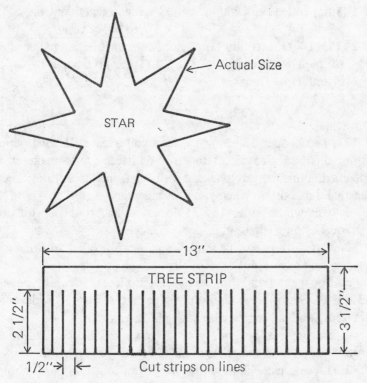

Actual Size

STAR

13"

TREE STRIP

2 1/2"

3 1/2"

1/2"

Cut strips on lines

Coat uncut edge of tree strip
with rubber cement on both sides

MERRY SANTA GIFT PACKAGE

For color photo, see Plate 4

Materials:

1 (1 lb.) coffee can with plastic lid

2 (17×14″) sheets thin white paper, such as layout paper from art supply store

Pink construction paper

3″ red bulky yarn

Blue construction paper

1 (10 oz.) red paper cup

Directions:

You need paper 13″ long to wrap coffee cans. If your paper is not this big, glue pieces together as necessary to make sizes specified. Finished gift package will fill from the bottom; keep plastic lid on bottom when you decorate can.

1. Cut white paper 13×3¼″ and wrap around bottom of can, overlapping edges; glue.

2. Cut pink paper 13×2¼″ and wrap around top of can, overlapping edges; glue.

3. For beard and hat trim, cut 8 pieces of white paper, 13×3½″. Slash paper along one edge into strips ½″ wide (see diagram) and curl strips with edge of scissors.

4. Starting at bottom, glue 5 rows of the curled paper around can, 1 over the other to make beard (see Step 1).

5. Trace mustache on white paper; cut out and paste above beard.

6. Glue red yarn in spiral to make round nose, and glue over mustache.

7. Cut 2 round blue eyes, ⅜″ diameter; glue in place.

8. Cover top of can with white paper (use plastic lid for pattern) and wrap rim with curled paper so that uncut edge extends above can about 1″ (see Step 2).

MERRY SANTA GIFT PACKAGE

YARN NOSE →

MUSTACHE

Actual Size

13"

2 1/2"

3 1/2"

← 1/2"

Cut strips   (Make 8)

2 curled strips →

Upside down paper cup →

Can Bottom →

Pink →

White →

Step 1.

Hat Trim →

Step 2.

9. Coil remaining 2 curled paper strips, 1 inside the other, to make a pompon. Glue to inside of rim at bottom of paper cup. Glue cup to paper on top of can.

10. Fill can from bottom with cookies or candies. Cover with plastic lid.

SILVER GIFT BOX

For color photo, see Plate 4

Materials:
   1 purchased foil-covered gift box (any size)
   Gold braid
   Self-adhesive silver bow

Directions:
   1. Glue gold braid to box in such a way that box can be opened and closed without disturbing decoration.
   2. Stick bow to lid of box.
   3. Line box with plastic bag. Fill with assorted candies, cookies, homemade mixes, or cereal treat. Top with decorated lid.

FLORAL GIFT TAG

For color photo, see Plate 7

Materials:
   1 (4¼×2½″) piece green felt
   1 (4¼×3″) piece heavy white paper or poster board

   8½″ yellow jumbo rickrack
   12 pumpkin seeds
   2 popcorn kernels
   Green felt-tip pen

Directions:

1. Glue felt to paper, leaving space at bottom for name.

2. Cut rickrack in half. Glue 1 piece along top edge of card. Glue other piece along bottom edge of felt.

3. Decorate felt with 2 daisies made from pumpkin seeds (6 petals each), centered with a popcorn kernel. Use tweezers to position them; glue in place. Draw stems and leaves with green felt pen.

4. Write name on card and use as a gift tag on a box of home-made goodies.

GIFT CANISTERS

For color photo, see Plates 1 & 4

Materials:
    Round containers
    Gift wrap or self-adhesive plastic, such as Con-Tact
    Ribbons and bows

Directions:

1. Choose any container that will hold the food you want to package. In our photos, we used coffee and shortening cans, a 12 oz. plastic container for frozen juice concentrate and an orange panty hose container.

2. Cover printing on containers with plain or patterned gift wrap or self-adhesive plastic. To determine length of paper needed, wrap string around circumference of canister; measure string; add ½" for overlap.

3. Decorate plain papers with gold foil seals or honeycomb plastic ribbon (from hobby stores—it's used for weaving place mats). Decorate lids with stick-on bows.

CLOWN TRAY FAVOR

For color photo, see Plate 7

Materials:

1 (9¼ × 3″) piece heavy
  white paper or poster
  board
Gold felt fabric
1 (1½″) Styrofoam ball
Red construction paper

2 small glitter trim eyes
Red curl sheen ribbon
Purple construction paper
Red print fabric (3 × 2½″)

Directions:

1. Fold cardboard on dotted lines to make tent shape (see diagram); glue.

2. From gold felt, cut rectangle 2¾ × 2½″. Glue to tent front.

3. Cut ball in half to make clown face. Trace nose and mouth on red paper; cut out and glue to face, along with eyes.

4. Cut 6 pieces of ribbon 2½″ long. Curl with edge of scissors; glue 3 curls on each side of clown face.

5. Trace hat on purple paper and glue to back of face.

6. Cut bow tie from red print fabric. Glue tie and face to gold felt.

7. Place clown tent on sick tray for child or attach to top of package.

CLOWN TRAY FAVOR

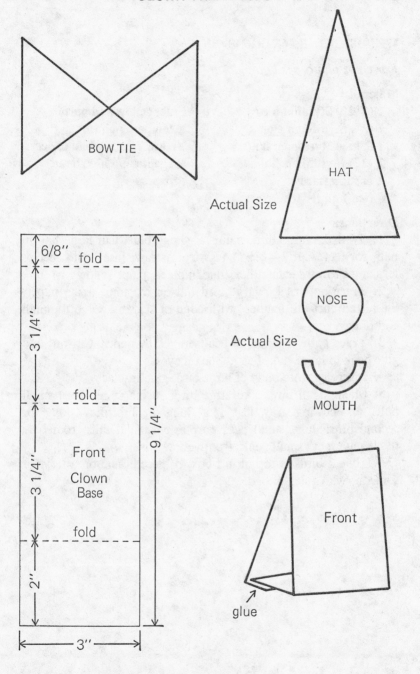

BOW TIE

HAT

Actual Size

NOSE

Actual Size

MOUTH

6/8" fold

3 1/4"

fold

Front
Clown
Base

9 1/4"

3 1/4"

fold

2"

3"

Front

glue

WHIMSICAL EGG BIRDS

For color photo, see book jacket

Materials:

1 (2½″) Styrofoam egg
2 (2″) Styrofoam eggs
1 (1½″) Styrofoam ball
2 (1″) Styrofoam balls
2 drinking straws
6 (½″) glitter trim eyes

Blue, yellow and purple
  tempera paint
Yellow construction paper
Magenta and blue tissue
  papers

Directions:

1. To make large bird, paint large egg blue. Cut large ball in half, for feet. Cut 2 (2½″) legs from straw; insert into feet so legs angle toward each other; glue in place; paint yellow.

2. Trace pattern for large bird tail on magenta tissue paper. Slash and curl tail feathers with edge of scissors. Glue to small end of egg.

3. Trace pattern for large beak on yellow paper. Cut out and glue beak to large end of egg; glue on eyes.

4. Insert legs into body of large bird; glue in place.

5. Make small birds like large birds, using small eggs, small balls, and cutting straw legs 1½″ long for 1 bird; 2″ long for second bird. Paint small eggs purple; cut small tails from blue tissue paper; cut small beaks from yellow paper.

6. Glue 3 birds to top of gift box, or perch them on a tray for someone who's sick in bed.

WHIMSICAL EGG BIRDS

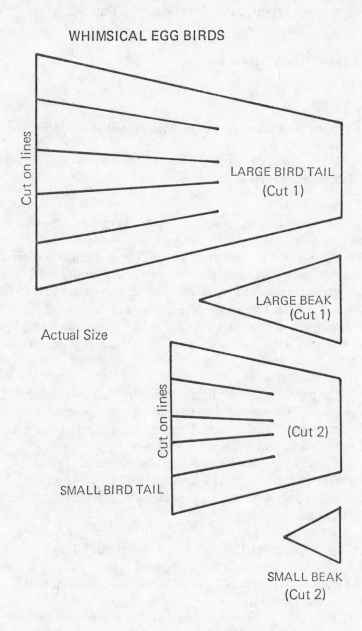

Cut on lines

LARGE BIRD TAIL
(Cut 1)

LARGE BEAK
(Cut 1)

Actual Size

Cut on lines

(Cut 2)

SMALL BIRD TAIL

SMALL BEAK
(Cut 2)

CASSEROLE CARRIER

For color photo, see Plate 7

Materials:
    ⅞ yard heavy cotton fabric (denim, sailcloth, poplin), 45″ wide*
    Cotton or polyester batting
    8 brass curtain rings

Directions:
* Or you can use fabric scraps, combining plain and patterned fabrics.

1. Mark and cut bias strips. You will need a finished piece 2″ wide, 60″ long. To cut bias: Fold fabric diagonally with crosswise grain parallel to lengthwise grain; the diagonal line of this fold is true bias. From this line, measure and mark off strips in parallel lines, 2″ wide (see Step 1). Cut strips. To join strips, lay end of 1 strip over the other, right sides together, so that the diagonal seam will be on straight grain of fabric (see Step 2). Stitch; press seam open.

2. On paper, with a string compass, draw a circle pattern 18″ in diameter. To make string compass, tie string around pencil. Tie other end of string around nail 9″ from pencil. Hold nail in center of paper and scribe circle with pencil (see Step 3).

3. Cut 2 (18″) circles of fabric. On straight of grain, cut 8 pieces 3×2″ for loops, and 2 pieces 30×2″ for handles.

4. Layer fabric pieces, right sides out, with batting between. Pin and quilt.

5. To make loops, fold 3″ sides to center and fold again, making a 4-layer strip 3×½″. Stitch down both sides.

6. Slip a ring on each strip and fold it over, making a loop. Sew loops to outer edge of quilted circle, spacing them evenly all around (see Step 4).

7. Bind edge of circle with bias strip (see Step 5).

CASSEROLE CARRIER

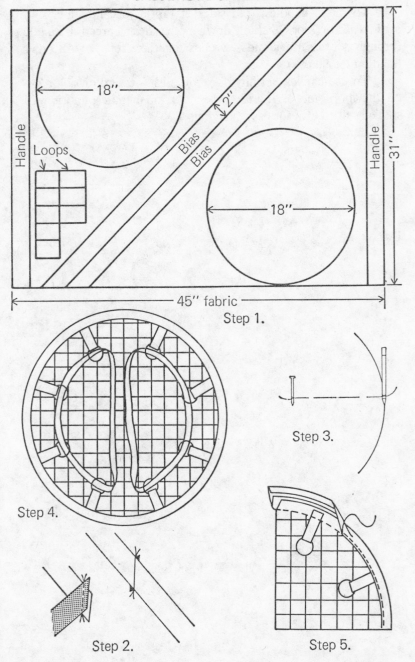

18"

2"

Bias
Bias

18"

Handle

Handle

Loops

31"

45" fabric

Step 1.

Step 4.

Step 3.

Step 2.

Step 5.

8. To make handles, fold sides of fabric to center and fold again (as for loops); stitch down both sides. Thread 1 handle through 4 brass rings and sew ends together; repeat with other handle (see Step 4).

9. To use carrier, set any casserole dish—round or oblong—on the loop side of fabric circle. Pick up handles; fabric will shape itself to dish for easy carrying.

INDEX